## DEDICATION

To my staff, without whom it would be
impossible to find the time to write a single word.

By the Same Author

*Pig Rearing & Health (Smallholder Practical Series)*
*First Catch Your Patient–A vet on Call*

# CONTENTS

# PREFACE

Veterinary surgeons spend at least five long years training for their chosen profession. This book is not meant to replace the vet in any way. It is intended to give the average farmer or smallholder a guide to disease recognition and treatment, the better to assist the vet when necessary.

The most important skill that a stock person must learn is the art of observation. Time spent looking over a gate just watching your stock is not mis-spent. Knowing what is normal behaviour in your own animals is vital. If you know what is normal then you will instantly know what is not. When you know the animal is behaving in an abnormal way you will then, with the aid of this book, or with the experience gathered over the years know how to react. You may feel competent, if the disorder is a minor one, to handle it for yourself. If in doubt get in touch with your vet. Vets are quite happy to proffer advice over the telephone and will know from the information you will have been able to impart, whether a visit is required.

It is at this point you must become systematic with your observations. Start at the head end and make a point of noting every little detail that you believe is abnormal. Make notes if necessary. For example, is the animal lame? If so on which leg is it lame? A useful, self evident fact about lameness is that the animal puts the lame leg to the ground for a shorter period of time than the other sound limbs. Buy a thermometer and learn how to use it properly. Your veterinary practice will help if you buy it from them.

Look for all obvious little things. A check list may be useful to mark the symptoms. This can be quite a simple affair and may be dispensed with when you become more experienced.

| | |
|---|---|
| EYES | Discharge/Yes/No/Purulent/Clear |
| EARS | Discharge/Yes/No/Swollen/Drooping |
| NOSE | Discharge/Yes/No/Purulent/Clear/Blood |
| MOUTH | Salivation/Yes/No/Ulcers |
| EATING | Yes/No |
| DRINKING | Yes/No |
| COUGH | Yes/No/Dry/Harsh/Soft |
| BREATHING | Fast/Slow |
| DIARRHOEA | Yes/No/Bloody/Mucus |
| VOMITING | Yes/No |
| CONSTIPATION | Yes/No |
| URINE | Retention/Yes/No/Dark/Bloody/Purulent |
| SKIN | Hair loss/Yes/No/Itch/Sores/Where present |
| LAMENESS | Yes/No  Which leg? |
| TEMPERATURE | High/Low |

This table gives an outline of what may be useful to the amateur diagnostician. It may be altered to suit individual needs and even although it may not allow the observer to reach a conclusion it will be of immense value to the veterinary surgeon to be able to describe the symptoms over the telephone if you are unsure whether a visit is required. Vets are still quite happy to give free advice over the phone to clients and should be able to decide from information received if further assistance is necessary.

If in doubt get the vet to call. It will be cheaper in the long run as it is much easier to treat and cure a patient in the early stage of a disease than later when it has become chronic problem.

Having made your provisional diagnosis, do not expect the vet to automatically dispense the drugs you think you may require.

The sale of medicines is regulated by the Medicines Act of 1968. This Act puts medicines into different categories and lays down guidelines for their dispensing, use and safe storage.

1. P.O.M. - Prescription only medicines. Medicines in this category, which include all the antibiotics, hormones, steroids and many other potent drugs, can only be prescribed by a veterinary surgeon. They may be sold by a vet or sold by a pharmacist on the receipt of a prescription from a vet. A vet may only prescribe or sell the P.O.M. medicine to a client whose animals are under his care. This care must be real and not nominal and the vet must have either seen the animal for which they are prescribing or have visited the farm sufficiently frequently to have personal knowledge of the health status of the farm.

Veterinary surgeons failing to comply with these regulations can find themselves in serious trouble with the authorities. No vet I know would take the risk of flouting the rules when the possible penalty, if discovered, is to be struck off the Register of Veterinary Surgeons and disbarred from practising. If you do obtain medicines, you will be required to make a record of the drug purchased and its subsequent use on the patient. The name or number of the animal has to be recorded, the medicine, the dose used and the withdrawal period before the animal can be sent for slaughter.

2. P.M.L. - Merchant List Drugs. The medicines in this category are mostly worming and other antiparasitic preparations and can be sold and dispensed by vets to their clients only. These medicines can also be purchased through registered merchants.

3. G.S.L. - General Sale List. medicines in this category, usually vitamins and minerals, can be obtained through any outlet that cares to stock them.

# CATTLE

The most assured way of trying to maintain the health of a breeding herd of cattle, providing housing and feeding are of a good standard, is to try to avoid buying in young untested animals to increase the herd. A bull may be brought in with little risk providing it comes from a known source whose health status is assured. Consider also using artificial insemination and/or embryo transplantation as a means of introducing new blood into the herd with no health risks.

If your business demands the purchase of calves, try to obtain them directly from the farm where they were born as market calves are subject to all manner of infections and stress. These incomers could seriously compromise the health of a breeding herd.

No matter how small a herd you might have, it is essential you have adequate facilities on hand with which to catch and restrain either the individual that may require examination or the whole herd which may have to be blood tested for Brucellosis or skin tested for Tuberculosis. Cattle stocks or crushes can be expensive if bought new but can be obtained more reasonably second hand. Possession of stocks and a race, which can be made temporarily with gates, is a necessity for safe handling of cattle both from the animals' point of view as well the handler. The only exceptions to this rule are if you are dealing only with youngsters or where dairy cattle are housed in individual stalls and are used to being handled very regularly.

# A GUIDE TO ANIMAL AILMENTS AND TREATMENT — CATTLE

| SIGNS OF DISEASE | CAUSES | TREATMENT AND PREVENTION |
|---|---|---|
| **HEAD AND FACE** | | |
| Nasal discharge. | Pneumonia due to bacterial, viral or parasitic infection. | Antibiotic for bacterial infection. Wormers for parasitic infection. If indoors, check ventilation. Vaccinate where appropriate. |
| Ulcers on lips, mouth and tongue. | Mucosal disease or Foot and Mouth NB NOTIFIABLE DISEASE. Malignant catarrh. | These are all due to virus infection. Antibiotic will control secondary bacterial infection. Control is through vaccination cleaning and disinfection and with Foot and Mouth in UK slaughter policy. |
| Salivation and drooling from mouth. | Ulcers, see above. Infection in tongue or mouth (lumpy jaw or wooden tongue). Obstruction in mouth or gullet eg choke due to potato or similar, or tumour. | Antibiotic for any general infection. Potassium iodide orally or sodium iodide intravenously. Remove foreign body if appropriate. Tumour/ slaughter on welfare grounds. |
| Loss of hair from face and muzzle. | Photosensitisation but only outdoors. | Move indoors, cortico steroids and antihistamines. |
| Loss of hair with scabs on face. | Ringworm. CARE, INFECTIOUS TO PEOPLE. | Antifungal/ topical or oral eg griseofulvin. |
| **EYES** | | |
| Discharge from both eyes. | Contagious infection eg New Forest Disease or symptom of more general infection eg malignant catarrhal fever or Mucosal Disease. | Topical eye treatment. General infection need antibiotic good nursing care, electrolytes. |
| Discharge from one eye. | Possible foreign body eg hay seed. May also be unilateral infection. | Remove foreign body. Apply topical antibiotic. |
| Swollen eye lids. | Allergic reaction. | Antihistamines or corticosteroids. |

10

| SIGNS OF DISEASE | CAUSES | TREATMENT AND PREVENTION |
|---|---|---|
| Eyes dull and lifeless. | General debility due to disease or deficiency. | Check for other symptoms. Treat general symptoms. |
| Blindness. | Cataracts. Pus or blood in eye due to trauma or infection. Lead poisoning. Vitamin deficiencies eg Vitamin A or Thiamine. | Nothing practical can be done. Some traumatic damage will repair. Calcium versenate. Give vitamins. |
| Yellow with colour in white of the eye. | Jaundice due to infection of liver or liver damage due to poisoning, eg Ragwort, or tumour. Redwater Fever (Babesiosis). | Antibiotic and vitamins. Good nursing and carbohydrate diet.<br><br>Endoparasite treatment. Eradicate. Ticks from pasture. |
| Mucosa of eye pale or white. | Anaemia due to worms or deficient diet. | Improve diet/ give iron. Deworm with anthelmintic. Check for cobalt or copper deficiency. |
|  | Poisoning eg bracken or Brassica. Redwater Fever due to Babesia infection. | Remove source of poison. Use endoparasiticide for Babesia infection. Eradicate Ticks from pasture. Vaccine may be available soon. |
| Mucosa of eye dark and congested. | Circulatory problem as part of a more generalised disease eg pneumonia. | Treat general disease/ check for other symptoms/ seek veterinary help. |
| Eyes sunk into eye sockets. | Dehydration usually as the result of scouring. | Check for cause of scour. Electrolytes and fluid replacement/ drip may be required. Antibiotic if infection present. |
| **EARS** One or both ears swollen. | Abscess or blood blister due to badly applied ear tag or other injury. | Drain abscess/ leave haematoma. May require topical antibiotic treatment. |
| One ear drooping/ pus discharging. | Infection eg Listeriosis. | Antibiotic eg oxytetracycline for Listeria infection. Make better silage. |
| **SKIN AND HAIR** Coat colour changes without hair loss. | Copper/zinc (rare) cobalt/manganese deficiency. | Blood samples required to confirm diagnosis before treatment of deficiency. Anthelmintic for worms. |

| SIGNS OF DISEASE | CAUSES | TREATMENT AND PREVENTION |
| --- | --- | --- |
| Loss of coat without itch. | Parasitic gastroenteritis (gut worms). Rain scald due to Dermatophilus infection. | Antibiotics eg oxytetracycline and penicillin/streptomycin. Improve housing conditions. |
| Loss of hair with round raised crusty lesions. | Ringworm. CARE INFECTIOUS TO PEOPLE. | Topical antifungal agents or oral griseofulvin. |
| Loss of hair with itching. | Ectoparasites eg lice or mange mites. | Skin scrapings may be required to confirm mange infection. Louse powders and mange washes. Pour on preparations eg ivermectin. |
| Raised sore areas in unpigmented part of coat. | Photosensitisation due to sunlight. Animal often becomes sensitive by eating plants such as St John's Wort or Rape. | House indoors/ treat with antihistamines, corticosteroids and sun blocking creams. Remove offending plants. |
| Growths on skin surface. | Warts or Angleberries. | Some warts go away spontaneously. Autogenous vaccine can be made for severe lesions. Surgery may be required for large lumps/ see vet. |
| Soft swellings on back. | Warble fly (no rare). | Ecto parsitical preparations (pour on and injectable). |
| **BREATHING** Rapid breathing. | Pneumonia due to viral bacterial or parasitic infection eg lungworms. | Antibiotic and anti-inflammatory drugs. Anthelmintic for lungworm. Vaccine for prevention. Get expert of check ventilation. |
| | Stress as the result of pain or overheating or exercise. | Remove source of stress. |
| | Heart disease or clot in main vein to heart. | Casualty slaughter may be only solution. |
| | Fog Fever (see below). | Corticosteroids. |
| Shallow breathing. | Asleep or Hypocalcaemia if recumbent (milk fever). | Check for other symptoms. Calcium injection usually effective. (subcutaneous or intravenous). |
| | Terminal stage of any illness. | |

| SIGNS OF DISEASE | CAUSES | TREATMENT AND PREVENTION |
|---|---|---|
| Coughing. | Symptom of respiratory disease eg pneumonia due to virus, bacteria or lungworm. | Antibiotic/ anti-inflammatory and mucolytic drugs. Anthelmintic for lungworm. |
| | Foreign material in windpipe due to incorrect dosing or drenching. | Inhalation pneumonia/ little can be done apart from antibiotic for infection. |
| | Fog Fever due to intoxication with L-tryphtophan. Occurs in Autumn on lush grazing. | Corticosteroids and anti-inflammatory drugs may help. Remove cattle from lush grazing. |
| **TEMPERATURE** Normal range is 101.5-102.5 F. | | |
| Raised. | Usually means animal has infection but may be the result of pain or stress. | Antibiotic required for most infections. Check for other symptoms. Pain killers may be necessary. If high temperature persists get advice. |
| Lowered. | Check reading again may be incorrect technique/ hypothermia or terminally ill. | If correct, raise body temperature with heat lamps or equivalent/ get advice. |
| Sweating. | See above for raised temperature. | See above for raised temperature. |
| Shivering. | See above for lowered temperature. | See above for lowered temperature. |
| **DUNG** Constipation. | Indigestion and reduced feed intake. | Check diet and for other symptoms. |
| | Acetonaemia. | Corticosteroids, intravenous glucose, vitamins, propylene glycol. |
| Scouring. | Nuturitional eg too much rich grass. | Feed hay before turning out. |
| | Bacterial infection eg Johne's Disease. | Antibiotic but no treatment for Johne's Disease. |

| SIGNS OF DISEASE | CAUSES | TREATMENT AND PREVENTION |
| --- | --- | --- |
| | Virus infection eg Mucosal disease/ Malignant catarrhal fever/ Infectious Bovine Rhino-tracheitis. | Antibiotic to cover secondary infection, fluid and supportive therapy. |
| | Parasites eg worms/fluke/coccidia | Anthelmintic. |
| | Plant or other poisoning. | Find and remove source of poison and treat symptoms. |
| Scouring with blood. | Salmonellosis (CARE, INFECTIOUS TO PEOPLE). Coccidiosis. Vibrionic (Campylobacter) scour. | Antibiotic/fluid therapy/good nursing. Oral antibiotic. All above require good hygienic precautions. Some types of Salmonella can be vaccinated against. |
| | Cancer. | Slaughter on welfare grounds. |
| Abdominal distension with fluid. | Pregnant. Heart disease. Peritonitis. | Get vet to confirm. Poor prognosis. May respond to antibiotic but generally poor outlook. |
| Abdominal distension left side abdomen ie bloat. | Gas not being belched from rumen. Due to obstruction eg potato or failure in nervous mechanism which allows belching or frothy bloat where gas and fluid are mixed as forth. | Remove foreign body or push it down into rumen. Pass stomach tube to relieve simple bloat. Drench with cooking oil or linseed oil to relieve frothy bloat. Chronic cases can be cured by vet making a permanent fistula. |
| | Impaction as the result high fibre diet. | Check diet in all cases. |
| Bloat with distention on both sides of abdomen. | Severe bloat, animal will be near to death. | May require emergency trocarisation. Get vet as soon as possible. |
| Urinary retention or inability to pass urine ie urolithiasis. | Calculi in urethra may cause partial or total blockage. | Muscle relaxant drugs may be all that is required in cases of partial blockage. Complete blockage required immediate attention and often surgery/ see vet urgently. |

| SIGNS OF DISEASE | CAUSES | TREATMENT AND PREVENTION |
|---|---|---|
| | Due to dietary imbalance of mineral usually magnesium. | Check diet/ add salt to diet as prevention. |
| Blood in urine. | Cystitis Bacterial infection eg Clostridial or Leptospiral infection. Kidney infection. | Antibiotic for routine infection in bladder and kidney. Vaccine can be used to prevent Clostridial or Leptospiral infection. |
| | Brassica/ bracken poisoning. Nitrite poisoning. | Antibiotic and drip to treat bracken cases/ same for Brassica cases plus vitamins and iron. Remove source of poison. Methylene blue solution for nitrite cases. |
| | Red Water Fever result of infection with Babesia. | Endoparasiticides/ blood may be required/ eradicate ticks from pasture. |
| Pain in abdomen; seen as lying down and getting up frequently, teeth grinding and kicking while lying down. | Colic due to intestinal inflammation or obstruction. Urolithiasis (see above). Peritonitis. Lead poisoning. | Muscle relaxant and pain killing drugs may be all that is required. Severe blockages, eg twisted bowel or urolithiasis, requires surgery. Antibiotic, poor outlook. Calcium versenate. |
| | Foreign body in rumen penetrating into liver and chest. | Surgery to retrieve foreign material/ successful if carried out early. |
| Swelling at navel | Rupture | Surgery rarely indicated. Usually better, unless animal is very valuable, to go for economic slaughter. |
| Fluid swelling along from udder | Udder oedema if just prior to or after calving | No treatment usually indicated. Swelling will go after a few days. |
| Fluid along brisket and abdoment. | Heart failure which may be primary or due to foreign body penetration from abdomen. | Diuretics may be helpful in minor cases but seldom practical. |
| **INFERTILITY** FEMALE Failure to come into season. | Pregnant or failure to detect season or low body weight or deficiency disease eg copper, manganese. Infection eg Brucellosis Ovarian problems. eg persistent corpus luteum. | Vet required to check for any possible pregnancy. All other conditions require correct diagnosis before vet can apply correct treatment. |
| | Congenital eg freemartinism. | Cull from herd. |

| SIGNS OF DISEASE | CAUSES | TREATMENT AND PREVENTION |
|---|---|---|
| Abortion. | Infection eg Brucellosis and Leptospirosis (CARE, BOTH INFECTIOUS TO PEOPLE). Any disease which causes rise in temperature eg virus or bacteria. Fungal infection. Clumsy management and poor handling. | Brucellosis is NOTIFIABLE DISEASE cull from herd. Leptospiral infection use antibiotic and can vaccinate. Investigate cause of abortion by blood test and swabs before attempting treatment. Good hygiene essential at all times and isolate cow until cause of abortion is known. |
| | Inadvertent injection of steroid or prostaglandin. | **BE MORE CAREFUL** |
| Vaginal discharge. Clear/with or without blood stain. | If pregnant may be about to give birth. Slight discharge can be apparent when in season. | Get experienced help to check. If in season will be behavioural signs. |
| Purulent smelly discharge with or without afterbirth being retained. | Primary infection in genital tract or due to retained afterbirth which may be hanging from vulva. | Antibiotic either by injection or by inserting pessaries or by irrigation. Remove afterbirth. |
| **INFERTILITY** MALE | Specific infection eg Brucellosis. Deficiency diseases eg Iodine, Manganese or Vit A. Orthopaedic problems eg sore back, legs or pelvis. | Infertility difficult to diagnose. Will require sperm counts and blood tests. Get vet to check and treat any lameness. |
| **MASTITIS** Blood in milk. Milk very thick after calving. | Just after calving can be quite normal. Colostrum. | No treatment required, will resolve in a day or two. Normal, no action required. Will clear in a day or two. |
| Clots in milk. | Milk form of mastitis due to infection by Streptococcus. | Antibiotic. Check bacterial sensitivity before treatment. Management may be at fault. |
| Watery milk. | Possible coliform mastitis. | Antibiotic as above. |
| Udder very hot and cow ill. | Severe mastitis possible C. pyogenes or Summer mastitis. | Antibiotic both in the udder and by injection. May require emergency vet treatment to save life. |

16

| SIGNS OF DISEASE | CAUSES | TREATMENT AND PREVENTION |
|---|---|---|
| Milk drop. | Leptospira or Mycoplasma infection. Mastitis. | Investigate before treatment with antibiotic. |
| Teat abnormalities. | Virus infection eg herpes or cow pox. Chapped or eroded teat ends. | Bland ointments/ udder cream. Check milking machine and management. |
| **LAMENESS** Feet | Interdigital infection eg Foul in the Foot or puncture wound. | Antibiotics/ may need to pare away the infected part. |
| | Septic arthritis in the foot joint. | Surgery may be required, see vet. |
| | Laminitis due to overeating. | Analgesics, warm water bathing to improve circulation. Methionine in diet may be helpful. |
| | Virus infection ie Foot and Mouth Disease (rare). | NOTIFIABLE DISEASE, CALL VET. |
| Limbs. | Injury eg fracture, nerve damage, puncture wounds and sprains. | All but most minor need vet attention. Treat symptoms. |
| | Arthritis. | Analgesics and anti-inflammatory drugs. Antibiotic. |
| | Joint infections. Blackleg due to Clostridial infection of the muscle. | High doses of antibiotic and Clostridial antiserum. Poor prognosis. Good vaccine available. |
| **BEHAVIOUR** Loss of appetite. | Any factor which causes a rise in temperature. Pain. | Check for other symptoms; look in mouth for sores and blisters. Fluids, glucose, corticosteroids. |
| | Acetonaemia due to negative energy balance (poor feeding management). | Improve feeding management. |
| | Acidosis due to gorging on carbohydrate. | Electrolytes, multivitamins antihistamines. |
| | Indigestion due to dysfunction of the vagus nerve. | Poor prognosis, treat symptoms, stomach drenches stimulants and good nursing. |

| SIGNS OF DISEASE | CAUSES | TREATMENT AND PREVENTION |
|---|---|---|
| Nervous signs eg blindness, head pressing, staggering gait, excitement. | Hypomagnesaemia (low blood magnesium). Milk Fever (low blood calcium). Lead poisoning usually from licking old paint. | Magnesium sulphate (subcutaneous injection) and sedation. Calcium borogulconate (intravenous subcutaneous injection). Calcium versenate injection/ (job for vet). Get rid of source of old paint. |
| | Nervous signs of acetonaemia. | See above. |
| | Listeriosis ie micro-abscesses in the brain. | Antibiotic. |
| | Louping Ill due to virus infection. | No specific treatment. remove bracken as source of tick/ vaccine is available. |
| Nervous signs eg walking in circle. | Gid (parasitic tape worm cyst on brain) or brain abscess or brain tumour or haemorrhage. | Surgical removal of cyst. Worm dogs as they carry the tapeworm. Slaughter on welfare grounds may be necessary. |
| Nervous signs eg any change in normal behaviour, aggression, anxiety, unsteady on legs. | Bovine Spongiform Encephalopathy (BSE). | NOTIFIABLE DISEASE. Slaughter policy. |
| Nervous signs eg convulsions and collapse. | Hypomagnesaemia see above. Terminal signs of any nervous disease. | See above. Euthanasia may be required on welfare grounds. |
| **RECUMBENCY** ie unable to stand and walk. | Milk Fever due to low blood calcium levels. | Calcium borogluconate by subcutaneous or intravenous injection. |
| | Downer cow syndrome/ often follows milk fever/ nerve and muscle damage. | Good nursing, stimulants, sling or lift patient with air bags. |
| | Physical injury. | Good nursing, treat symptomatically. |
| | Terminal stages of any fatal illness. | May require euthanasia on welfare grounds. |

| SIGNS OF DISEASE | CAUSES | TREATMENT AND PREVENTION |
|---|---|---|
| **SUDDEN DEATH** | Anthrax (NOTIFIABLE DISEASE AND INFECTIOUS TO PEOPLE). | All sudden deaths must be checked by law. Get vet OR INFORM LOCAL DIVISIONAL VETERINARY OFFICER. |
| | Bloat (see above). Plant poisoning eg Yew, Laburnum, Laurel. Any Clostridial infection eg Black leg. Hypomagnesaemia. Lightning strike or Electrocution. | NEVER LEAVE HEDGE OR TREE CLIPPINGS WHERE ANIMAL CAN REACH Vaccines are available and effective<br><br>Prevent with supplements or Bolus Scorch marks may be seen on skin. GET QUALIFIED PERSON TO CHECK WIRING. |

# A GUIDE TO ANIMAL AILMENTS AND TREATMENT — CALVES

| SIGNS OF DISEASE | CAUSES | TREATMENT AND PREVENTION |
|---|---|---|
| **HEAD AND FACE** | | |
| Nasal discharge. | Pneumonia/bacteria virus/parasites. | Antibiotics for infection, wormers for lung worm. Check ventilation. Vaccinate where appropriate. |
| Ulcers on lips and mouth. | Pox virus/mucosal disease/Foot and Mouth/ malignant catarrhal fever. | Antibiotic for secondary infection. Foot and Mouth is a NOTIFIABLE DISEASE. |
| Salivation and drooling from mouth. | Ulcers, see above. Infection in tongue or mouth eg calf diphtheria. | Antibiotics for any infection. |
| | Obstruction in mouth or gullet. | Remove foreign body eg potato if appropriate. |
| Loss of hair from face/muzzle. | Photosensitisation but only outdoors. | Move indoors, steroids and antihistamines. |
| | Vitamin A deficiency in milk fed calves. | Give vitamins until calf is eating creep feed. |
| Loss of hair with scabs on face. | Ringworm. CARE INFECTIOUS TO PEOPLE. | Antifungal/topical and oral eg griseofulvin. |
| Loss of hair around mouth. | Milk scald due to bucket feeding. | Will resolve when bucket feeding stops. |
| **EYES** | | |
| Discharge from both eyes. | Contagious infection eg New Forest disease or symptom of more general infection eg pneumonia. | Treat with antibiotic in eyes or if more general by injection. |
| Discharge from one eye | Possible foreign body eg hay seed or straw. | Remove. |
| | Turned in eye lid. | Minor operation required see vet. |
| Swollen eye lids. | Allergic reaction. | Antihistamines or corticosteroids. |
| Eyes dull and lifeless. | Part of general disease eg pneumonia or scours. | Treat general symptoms. |

| SIGNS OF DISEASE | CAUSES | TREATMENT AND PREVENTION |
|---|---|---|
| Blindness. | Congenital cataracts. | Nothing can be done. |
| | Lead poisoning. | Calcium versenate. |
| | Vitamin deficients eg Vit A or thiamine. | Give vitamins. |
| | Infection. | Antibiotics. |
| Yellow colour in white of eye. | Jaundice due to liver disease or liver damage. | Antibiotics and vitamins. High carbohydrate diet. |
| Mucosa of eye pale or white. | Anaemia due to worms or deficient diet. | Improve diet/ give iron/ kill worms with anthelmintic. |
| Mucosa of eye dark and congested. | Circulation problem as part of more general disease eg pneumonia. | Treat general disease/ see vet. |
| Eyes sunk into eye sockets. | Dehydration, usually caused by scouring. | Electrolytes as fluid replacers/ antibiotics if infection present. |

**EARS**

| | | |
|---|---|---|
| One or both ears swollen. | Abscess or blood blister due to badly applied ear tag or injury. | Drain abscess/ leave haematoma/ vet to decide treatment. |
| One ear drooping/ pus discharging. | Infection/ possible Listeriosis. | Antibiotics eg oxytetracycline. |

**SKIN AND HAIR**

| | | |
|---|---|---|
| Coat colour changes without hair loss. | Copper/zinc (rare) cobalt/maganese deficiency. | Blood samples required for diagnosis before treatment for deficiencies. |
| | Parasitic gastroenteritis (gut worms). | Anthelmintic for worms. |
| Loss of coat without itch. | Rain scald due to Dermatophilus infection. | Antibacterial and improve housing conditions. |
| Loss of coat with round raised crusty lesions. | Ringworm. CARE INFECTIOUS TO PEOPLE. | Topical antifungal agents and oral griseofulvin. |
| Loss of coat with itching. | Ectoparasites eg lice or mange mites. | Louse powders/mange washes/ pour on preparations eg ivermectin. |

| SIGNS OF DISEASE | CAUSES | TREATMENT AND PREVENTION |
|---|---|---|
| Raised sore areas in unpigmented part of coat. | Photosensitisation due to sunlight Animal has to be sensitised by eating plants such as St John's Wort or Rape. | House indoors/ treat with antihistamines, corticosteroids and sun blocking creams. |
| Growths on skin surface. | Warts or Angleberries. | Most wart resolve spontaneously. Autogenous vaccine can be made for severe lesions. Surgery may be required/ see vet. |

## BREATHING

| | | |
|---|---|---|
| Rapid breathing. | Pneumonia due to virus,. bacteria or parasites eg lungworms. | Antibiotic and anti-inflammatory drugs. Anthelmintic for lungworm. Vaccinate to prevention. |
| | Stress due to pain or overheating or exercise. | Get expert to check environment. Remove source of stress. |
| Shallow breathing. | Asleep or in terminal stage of illness. | No action. Check for other symptoms/ get vet. |
| Coughing. | Respiratory disease eg pneumonia due to bacteria/ virus or parasite. | Antibiotics, anti-inflammatory agents and mucolytics. See vet. |
| | Foreign material in windpipe due to bad drenching or dosing. | Remove foreign body if possible antibiotics for secondary infection. |

## TEMPERATURE
Normal range is
101.5 - 102.5F.

| | | |
|---|---|---|
| Raised. | Usually means infection but may be the result of stress or pain. | Antibiotic for infection/ remove source of stress/. Analgesics for pain. See vet. |
| Lowered. | Check again, incorrect technique or hypothermia or terminally ill. | If correct, raise body temperature with heat lamps or equivalent/ get advice. |
| Sweating. | See above for raised temperature. | See above for raised temperature. |
| Shivering. | See above for lowered temperature. | See above for lowered temperature. |

| SIGNS OF DISEASE | CAUSES | TREATMENT AND PREVENTION |
|---|---|---|
| **DUNG** | | |
| Constipation. | Rarely a problem. | Check diet. |
| Scouring. | Milk scour due to overfeeding. | Stop or reduce milk intake and give electrolytes. |
| | Bacterial infection eg E. coli or Salmonella (CARE INFECTIOUS TO PEOPLE). | Antibiotics for bacterial infections/ good general nursing care eg keep clean and warm. |
| | Virus or coccidial infection. | Vaccines may help control virus infections. |
| | Consider possible worm infestation if out at grass. | Anthelmintic to get rid of worm burden. |
| Scouring with blood. | Salmonella infection likely if very depressed. | Antibiotics and a high standard of nursing care is required. |
| | Coccidiosis. | Coccidiostat normally very effective. |
| Bloat. ie abdominal distension of the left side abdomen. | Gas not being belched from rumen. Due either to obstruction in the gullet or failure in the mechanism to allow belching or frothy bloat where gas and fluid are mixed as a froth. | Remove foreign body from gullet. Pass stomach tube to relieve simple bloat. Drench with linseed oil or cooking oil to relieve frothy bloat. Check diet in all cases. |
| Bloat with distension on both sides of abdomen. | Severe bloat, animal will be close to death. | May require emergency trocarisation. Get vet as soon as possible. |
| **URINE** | | |
| Urinary retention or blockage. ie urolithiasis. | Calculi in urethra may cause partial or total blockage. Cause is usually dietary imbalance of mineral usually magnesium. | Relaxant drug may be all that is required in cases of partial blockage. Surgery often necessary/ see vet, urgently. For control add salt to diet. |
| Blood in urine. | Infection eg Clostridial or acute leptospiral disease. (rare) or Brassica poisoning eg Kale. | High doses of antibiotic required for infection. Stop feeding Brassica/ vitamin and iron injections. Severe cases may require blood transfusions. |

| SIGNS OF DISEASE | CAUSES | TREATMENT AND PREVENTION |
|---|---|---|
| Pain in abdomen; seen as lying down and getting up frequently, teeth grinding and kicking while lying down. | Colic due to intestinal inflammation or obstruction.<br><br>Urolithiasis (see above).<br><br>Peritonitis.<br><br>Lead poisoning. | Muscle relaxant drugs may be all that is required. Severe blockage eg twisted bowel or urolithiasis, require surgery.<br><br><br>Antibiotics, poor outlook.<br><br>Calcium versenate. Get vet. |
| Swelling at the navel. | Rupture.<br><br>Abscess at navel due to infection getting in at birth. | No action if small. Surgery indicated if swelling is large.<br><br>Antibiotic at high doses. May be difficult to clear. |
| Fluid lower belly. | Calculi in the urethra blocking the flow of urine. | Surgery almost always the only treatment. See vet. |
| **LAMENESS**<br>Feet. | Interdigital infection eg Foul in the Foot or puncture wound.<br><br>Laminitis due to overfeeding.<br><br>Virus infection ie Foot and Mouth (rare). | Antibiotics and may need to pare away the infected part.<br><br>Analgesics, warm water bathing to improve circulation. Methionine in the diet.<br><br>NOTIFIABLE DISEASE call vet. |
| Limbs. | Injury eg fracture, nerve damage, puncture wounds and strain. Joint ill ie infection.<br><br>Rickets.<br>If stiff and unable to rise, consider Vit E deficiency. | All but most minor need vet attention. Treat symptoms. Antibiotics as early as possible.<br><br>Calcium and vitamin D.<br>Vit E injections. |
| **BEHAVIOUR**<br>Loss of appetite. | Rise in temperature.<br>Pain. | Check for other symptoms; look in mouth for sores. |

| SIGNS OF DISEASE | CAUSES | TREATMENT AND PREVENTION |
| --- | --- | --- |
| Nervous signs eg walking in circles or head pressing. | Cerebrocortical necrosis (CCN) ie thiamine deficiency. | Inject thiamine (usually present in multivitamin preparations. Control with roughage in diet, plus Brewers grains. |
| | Lead poisoning usually from licking old paint. | Calcium versenate injection (job for vet). Get rid of source of old paint. |
| | Infection eg Listeriosis causing microabscesses in brain. | Antibiotic. Silage may be source of infection. |
| | Gid (parasitic tape worm cyst on brain) or brain abscess, brain haemorrhage or brain tumour. | Surgical removal of cyst. Worm dogs as they carry the tape worm. Slaughter on welfare grounds may be necessary. |
| Nervous signs eg convulsions. | Hypomagnesaemia due to a drop in blood magnesium. | Injections of magnesium with or without calcium. Sedative. |
| | Terminal signs of any nervous disease. | Euthanasia may be required on welfare grounds. |
| **SUDDEN DEATH.** | Anthrax (NOTIFIABLE DISEASE AND INFECTIOUS TO PEOPLE). Bloat/ see above Plant poisoning eg Yew, Laburnum, Laurel. | Get vet to check in all cases by doing a post mortem when necessary. DON'T LEAVE HEDGE OR TREE CLIPPINGS WHERE ANIMAL CAN REACH. |
| | Hypomagnesmia Lightning strike or Electrocution | Prevent with supplements or Bolus. Scorch marks may be seen on skin. GET QUALIFIED PERSON TO CHECK WIRING. |

# SHEEP

Sheep have always been a very important part of the agricultural economy and while traditional methods of husbandry are still employed, new management techniques, particularly with regard to breeding are revolutionising the sheep industry.

This does not mean that we can abandon tried and tested methods of looking after sheep without much thought and care for the possible consequences.

Sheep still die infuriatingly frequently, with only a slight froth on their lips to mark the manner of their passing.

This sudden death is often due to Clostridial infection of one type or another and the fact that good and effective vaccination has been available for many years to prevent such deaths does not seem to stop them happening. The cost of vaccination should rarely be a factor as the vaccine is relatively cheap. It should not be due to ignorance of the presence of Clostridial disease as these bacteria are always present in the soil and vaccine manufacturers advertise their products extensively. I tend to believe, in the absence of any other theory, that if the flock has had a trouble free existence for a period of years, then it is all too easy to want to cut corners and omit a vital injection. The consequences of so doing may not be apparent at the time, but dead sheep will be the result eventually.

Preventing disease with good husbandry and an effective vaccination programme makes good economic sense.

# A GUIDE TO ANIMAL AILMENTS AND TREATMENT — SHEEP

| SIGNS OF DISEASE | CAUSES | TREATMENT AND PREVENTION |
|---|---|---|
| **HEAD AND FACE** | | |
| Nasal Discharge. | Pneumonia due to virus or bacterial infection. Most common infection is due to Pasteurella. | Antibiotic for most cases. If indoors check ventilation. Vaccine available for prevention of Pasteurella. |
| | Watery discharge from nostrils may be due to Jaagsiekte (Pulmonary Adenomatosis). | No treatment. No vaccine available. |
| Nasal discharge with pus and blood. | Sheep Nasal fly. Seen only in the summer months. | Invermectin may be useful as can organophosphorous dips pour on insecticides. |
| Ulcers on lips, tongue and dental pad. | Foot and Mouth Disease (rare) NOTIFIABLE DISEASE. | Check for other symptoms eg blisters on feet. If suspicious inform vet or Ministry official. |
| Scabs around eyes, ears and base of horns. | Facial eczema or Eye Scab due to bacterial infection, Staph aureus. Head fly. | Antibiotic, usually injectable. Isolate affected animals and increase trough space Pour on insecticide. |
| | Photosensitisation may be a factor in summer months. | Eating St Johns Wort or clover may precipitate condition. Move to other pasture or indoors. Treat with steroids or antihistamines. |
| Loss of hair on face especially around the eyes. | Ringworm, usually due to Trychophyton verrucosum. Rare condition. CARE, INFECTIOUS TO PEOPLE. | Topical and oral antifungal agents eg Griseofulvin. |

| SIGNS OF DISEASE | CAUSES | TREATMENT AND PREVENTION |
|---|---|---|
| Salivation and drooling from the mouth. | Virus infection eg Foot and Mouth. See above. | See previous page. |
| | Actinobacillosis ie bacterial infection in the mouth, jaw bone and elsewhere. | Antibiotic or sodium iodide intravenous weekly or potassium iodide orally daily. |
| | Foreign body eg potato or other similar root stuck in mouth or throat. | Abdomen may be blowing up with gas. Emergency situation. If unable to dislodge or push into stomach it may be necessary to place trocar and canula in rumen to relieve bloat. |
| | Might have tooth problems or abscess or tumour. | Tumour; no treatment viable. Dental treatment may be available from the vet. |
| Fluid swelling under jaw. | Chronic fluke infection. | Routine treatment with fluke preparation used both as treatment and prevention. Drain land and try to get rid of the snail which is the intermediate host. |

**EYES**

| SIGNS OF DISEASE | CAUSES | TREATMENT AND PREVENTION |
|---|---|---|
| Watery discharge from one or both eyes. | Entropion ie inturned eye lid(s). Usually rectified as young animal. | Minor surgery required. See vet. |
| White discharge from one or both eyes sometimes with damage to the surface of the eye. | Infectious Kerato-conjunctivitis due to infection by Rickettsia or Chlamydia organism. | Subconjuntival injection (job for the vet) or topical antibiotic ointment. Control is difficult/ reduce crowding. |
| Discharge from one eye with or without eye damage. | Look for foreign body in the eye. eg hay seed or similar. | Careful search and remove after putting local anaesthetic in eye. Will need antibiotic eye ointment. |
| Swollen eye lids. | Allergic reaction. | Antihistamine or corticosteroid injections. May have to move pastures. |
| Eyes dull and lifeless. | Part of any general disease condition. eg Toxaemia. | Look for other symptoms before beginning treatment. If in doubt get vet. |

| SIGNS OF DISEASE | CAUSES | TREATMENT AND PREVENTION |
|---|---|---|
| Blindness with obvious eye lesions. | Cataracts. Damage to the surface after infection or trauma. | Nothing practical can be done. Topical antibiotic and steroid cream may be helpful. |
| Blindness with no obvious eye damage. | Rape or other Brassica poisoning. | Remove from field. |
| | Bracken poisoning. | Remove from source. Antibiotic and thiamine may help. |
| | Any form of brain degeneration caused by infection eg abscesses or toxaemia eg pregnancy Toxaemia. | Check for other symptoms to make a full diagnosis before beginning treatment. |
| Yellow colour in the white of the eye. | Jaundice usually the result of copper poisoning or chronic liver disease eg Fascioliasis. | Oral dose of sodium sulphate Prognosis is poor. Treat with fluke remedies. |
| Membranes of the eye pale or white. | Anaemia due to worms or fluke. | Treat with anthelmintic. |
| | Deficiency disease eg due to lack of copper, cobalt or iron in the diet. | Copper or cobalt boluses BUT ONLY AFTER A DEFINITE DIAGNOSIS HAS BEEN MADE BY BLOOD TESTING. |
| Membranes of the eye dark and congested. | Circulatory difficulties as part of more general disease eg pneumonia. | Check for other symptoms. If in doubt see vet. |
| Eyes sunk into sockets. | Dehydration usually as the result of scouring. | Electrolyte and fluid therapy and treat the cause of the scour. |
| **EARS** One or both ears swollen. | Abscess or blood blister ie haematoma. | Drain abscess and give antibiotic. Haematoma; leave to reabsorb naturally. |
| One ear drooping with possible discharge from one ear canal. | Bacterial infection or possible Listeriosis. | Antibiotic. If Listeriosis consider source of infection eg silage. Also practice good hygiene in lambing pen. |

| SIGNS OF DISEASE | CAUSES | TREATMENT AND PREVENTION |
|---|---|---|
| **SKIN AND FLEECE** | | |
| Loss of fleece with scabs and itching. | Sheep scab due to Psoroptic mite infection. Until recently NOTIFIABLE DISEASE. Now any untreated sheep with infection may be welfare cases and farmer prosecuted. | Dip with approved sheep scab dip. CARE: ENSURE ALL SAFETY PRECAUTIONS ARE OBSERVED WHEN DIPPING. |
| Severe itching with nervous symptoms. | Scrapie due to infection by a small virus - like particle. | No treatment. All infected animals should be slaughtered. |
| Loss of fleece with itching. Parasites found. | Lice, Ticks and Keds could all be involved. | Dip or spray or pour on affected animals with recommended products. This may have to be repeated every 10 to 14 days. |
| Wet staining of wool mostly around the rear end and with the animal distressed. | Blowfly maggots. | Dip or spray or pour on with recommended products affected and non-affected animals. Dag the flock ie clean or clip the area of the dock. Severely affected animals may have to be put down. |
| Discolouration of the fleece with crusting of the wool. No distress to the animal. | Dermatophilus infection; often common in cool wet weather. | Injectable antibiotic can be helpful. Keep animals dry. Alum dips may be helpful. |
| Wrinkled skin with sores. | Zinc deficiency. Rare condition. | Zinc sulphate weekly. Control with zinc fertiliser on pasture. |
| Total or partial loss of coat. No itching and no infection. | Wool slip. Not uncommon and thought due to hormonal factors. | No treatment. Protection from the worst of the weather may be necessary. |

| SIGNS OF DISEASE | CAUSES | TREATMENT AND PREVENTION |
|---|---|---|
| **BREATHING** | | |
| Rapid breathing. | Symptoms may be due to pain, over exercise or overheating. | Remove the source of the stress and the symptoms should resolve quite quickly. |
| | Pneumonia commonly due to bacterial infection eg Pasteurella. | Injectable antibiotic. Reduce stress, check ventilation if indoors. Vaccine available for Pasteurella infection. |
| | Parasitic pneumonia due to lung worm infection. Many species could be involved. | Anthelmintic required eg Ivermectin or Levamisole or Fenbendazole among others are effective. |
| | Jaagsiekte Pulmonary Adenomatosis due to virus infection. | No treatment available. Get stock from disease - free sources. |
| Shallow breathing. | Asleep or in terminal stage of illness. | Check for other symptoms and get vet as necessary. |
| Coughing. | Respiratory infection eg pneumonia due to infection bacteria, virus or Parasite. | Antibiotic, anti inflammatory drugs and mucolytics. Anthelmintic for lung worm. Get vet to check diagnosis. |
| | Inhalation pneumonia following faulty drenching of dosing. | Antibiotic to control secondary infection. Improve drenching technique. |
| **TEMPERATURE** Normal range is 101.5-102.5 F | | |
| Raised. | Usually means infection but may be the result of heat stress or pain. | Check for other symptoms. If in doubt check with the vet. Antibiotic for infection. Pain killers for pain. |
| Lowered. | Check again, may be incorrect technique or reading. If correct may be terminally ill. | Check for other symptoms eg diarrhoea. Give symptomatic treatment until a diagnosis is established eg warm patient up slowly. |
| **DUNG** | | |
| Constipation. | Uncommon but may be the sequel to digestion problems or fever. | Consider the primary cause of the problem and give laxative eg liquid paraffin or epsom salts in bran mash. |

| SIGNS OF DISEASE | CAUSES | TREATMENT AND PREVENTION |
|---|---|---|
| Scouring. | Parasitic gastro-enteritis ie worms many species may be involved. Faecal sample required to make diagnosis. | Dose with anthelmintic and move onto clean pasture. |
| | Chronic Fascioliasis ie chronic fluke infection. | Dose with anthelmintic preparation specifically for fluke see vet if in doubt. Drain land and get rid of snail which is the intermediate host. |
| Scouring, light in colour. | Ruminal acidosis due to animal having eaten too many concentrates or cereal. | Take off concentrate diet. Give bicarbonate by mouth. Multivitamins and antihistamines may help. |
| Dung persistently soft. | Johne's Disease due to infection by Mycobacterium johnei. | None. Slaughter all known cases. |
| Scouring after change of diet or moving onto new pasture. | Nutritional upset due to change of diet or lush pasture. | Increase roughage in diet eg hay and symptoms will disappear. |
| Scouring with retarded growth and wool reduced or straight without crimp. | Consider copper or cobalt deficiency. Need blood test for diagnosis. | Give copper or cobalt orally or by injection. |

## BLOAT

| | | |
|---|---|---|
| Bloat ie abdominal distention of left side of abdomen. | Gas not being belched from rumen. Could be due to obstruction in gullet eg by potato or failure in the mechanism to allow belching or Frothy Bloat (more common in adult sheep) where gas and stomach contents are mixed as a froth | If bloat due to obstruction remove it or push it down into the stomach. If this is not possible vet will usually insert trocar and cannula to relieve abdominal distention. If Frothy bloat use stomach drench of silicone or vegetable oil preparations. |
| | Frothy bloat usually caused by overeating especially on lucerne or clover. | Remove from suspect pasture or severely restrict access. |

| SIGNS OF DISEASE | CAUSES | TREATMENT AND PREVENTION |
|---|---|---|
| Bloat with distention on both sides of abdomen. | Severe bloat. Animal will be close to death. | May require emergency trocarisation get vet ASAP. |

**URINE**

| SIGNS OF DISEASE | CAUSES | TREATMENT AND PREVENTION |
|---|---|---|
| Urinary retention or blockage sometimes with distended abdomen. | Urolithiasis. Not common in adult sheep. Due to calculi blocking the urethra. | Muscle relaxant drugs can help if blockage is only partial. Surgery or euthanasia in severe cases. Salt in diet may be used as prevention. Check diet. |
| Discoloured urine often dark red in colour. | Clostridial infection. Animal usually collapsed due to toxaemia. | Antibiotic and fluid therapy. Poor prognosis. Vaccinate to prevent. |
| | Copper poisoning due to excessive intake. | Oral dose of sodium sulphate and ammonium molybdate may help. |
| | Rape or other Brassica poisoning. | Remove from source of trouble. Multivitamins may help. Feed hay before putting onto Brassica grazing and control amount grazed. |
| Pain in abdomen; seen as lying down and getting up frequently, teeth grinding and kicking while lying down. | Colic due to bloat, urolithiasis or intestinal torsion or blockage. | Muscle relaxants and pain killers may help plus see above. |
| | Clostridial infections can cause pain eg Pulpy Kidney. | Clostridial antisera and antibiotic. Vaccinate to prevent. |

**LAMENESS**

| SIGNS OF DISEASE | CAUSES | TREATMENT AND PREVENTION |
|---|---|---|
| Feet. | Bacterial infection in the foot eg foot abscess, Foot Rot or Foot Scald. Commonly due to Fusiformis species or if abscess, Corynebacteria. | Pare foot where appropriate and dress with topical antibiotic spray. Inject antibiotic where necessary. Keep on dry ground and use foot baths. |
| | Virus infection eg Foot and Mouth Disease. | Check for ulcers in mouth if in doubt call vet. NOTIFIABLE DISEASE. |

| SIGNS OF DISEASE | CAUSES | TREATMENT AND PREVENTION |
|---|---|---|
| Limbs. | Injury eg fracture, nerve damage, puncture wound or strain. | All but the most minor may need vet attention. Treat as required by symptoms. |
| | Clostridial infection eg Black Leg. | Large doses of antibiotic and antisera. Vaccinate to prevent. |
| | Specific joint infection eg Erysipelas or C pyogenes. | Antibiotic and good hygiene required. Clean pens and dips. |
| | Tick pyaemia due to Staph aureus abscesses in the joints and perhaps elsewhere. | Antibiotic. Tick control can help. |
| Reluctant to move on all limbs or just forelimbs. | Laminitis ie inflammation in the lamina of the foot, due to bacterial toxins in blood stream or may be just simply overweight. | Pain killing and anti-inflammatory drugs. Bathe feet in warm water. Reduce concentrate feed. |
| **INFERTILITY** FEMALE. Failure to come into season. | Pregnant. | Vet required to check for any possible pregnancy. |
| | Low body weight or deficiency disease eg Copper or Manganese. | Check diagnosis with blood samples before undertaking any treatment. |
| | Possible genital trace infection. | Antibiotic or cull from flock. |
| | Ovarian problems which if in young sheep may be congenital. | If treating individual it may be worth trying hormone treatment but if congenital problem cull from flock. |

| SIGNS OF DISEASE | CAUSES | TREATMENT AND PREVENTION |
|---|---|---|
| Abortion | Infection most likely cause eg Enzootic Abortion due to Chlamydia (CARE, CAN CAUSE SERIOUS INFECTION IN WOMEN). Toxoplasmosis, Border Disease, Campyloba cter, Listeriosis, Tick Borne Fever and Funal infections are the most common. | All abortions should be investigated with blood tests and swabs before attempting treatment. Good hygiene essential at all times. Vaccine available for prevention of Enzootic and Toxoplasmosis. Isolate affected animals until diagnosis is made. |
| | Isolated cases may be due to poor handling and clumsy management. | Check management. |
| Vaginal discharge. Clear with or without blood stain. | If pregnant, may be about to give birth. Slight discharge may be apparent when in season. | If shepherd in doubt - get vet to check. |
| Purulent, smelly discharge with or without afterbirth being retained. | May be primary infection in genital tract or due to retained afterbirth some of which may be hanging from vulva. Dead lamb(s) may still be retained in uterus. | Antibiotic by injection and or intro uterine pessaries or uterine irrigation. Remove retained afterbirth if possible and any retained lambs. |
| **INFERTILITY** MALE | Specific infection in the testicle(s). | Better to cull the animal than attempt treatment. |
| | Deficiency disease eg Vit A or Zinc. | Vitamin or Zinc supplements. |
| | Orthopaedic problems eg sore back or legs or pelvis making it difficult for the animal to mount. | Should be self evident to careful observation. Get vet to check and treat any lameness. |
| | Sores around sheath or scrotum may inhibit mating. Check for Orf. | Localised treatment with antibiotic may be helpful. |
| **MASTITIS** Milk very thick, immediately after lambing. | Normal/ colostrum. | No action required will clear in a day or two. |

| SIGNS OF DISEASE | CAUSES | TREATMENT AND PREVENTION |
|---|---|---|
| Clots in milk. | Mild form of mastitis. Many bacteria might be involved but probably a Streptococcus. | Intramammary antibiotic required. |
| Milk very watery and udder often very sore and red. | Acute mastitis due to E.coli or Pasteurella or Staphylococcus aureus. | Antibiotic both intramammary and injectable. |
| Udder cold, ewe very ill, blood stained fluid present at teat. | Per acute mastitis with gangrene. Usually due to Staph. aureus or Pasteurella infection. | May be necessary to amputate teat to allow drainage. Antibiotic, anti-inflammatory drugs and elctrolytes may be required. Grave prognosis. |
| Udder normal temperature but hard, no milk expressed. | Chronic mastitis. | Possibly no effective treatment but try antibiotic injection. Cull ewe before next lambing season. |
| | May be just blocked teat canal. | Get vet to check and unblock if possible. |
| Red sores over the udder area. | Orf ie virus infection. | Antibiotic may help. Vaccine available. |
| | Sheep Pox (rare) or Dermatophilus infection. | Antibiotic may be useful in both cases. |

**BEHAVIOUR**

| | | |
|---|---|---|
| Loss of appetite. | Any infection causing a rise in temperature. | Check for other symptoms before starting treatment. |
| | Pain; check mouth for sores eg Foot and Mouth blisters. Check for abdominal pain eg teeth grinding and grunting. | Treatment depending on cause of pain and definite diagnosis required - see vet. |
| Slow progressive loss of appetite in pregnant animal and finally recumbency. | Pregnancy toxaemia due to energy deficiency caused by faulty management. | Glycerol, propylene glycol orally, steroids and anabolic steroid. Abortion may be necessary to save ewe's life. Ensure adequate diet and exercise in last half of pregnancy. |

| SIGNS OF DISEASE | CAUSES | TREATMENT AND PREVENTION |
|---|---|---|
| Fairly sudden loss of appetite and then recumbency in later pregnancy and after lambing. | Hypocalcaemia/ lack of calcium in circulation. | Give calcium intravenously or under the skin. |
| Walking in circles and head pressing. | Middle ear infection or Listeriosis. | Antibiotic. Avoid silage feeding. Good hygiene essential. |
| | Gid (Sturdy) ie tape worm cyst in brain. | Surgery to remove cyst. Routine tape worm dosing of all dogs. |
| Head pressing with peculiar gait, then recumbency. | Louping Ill due to virus infection. | Antisera may be some use if used early. Vaccine available. Control tick which is intermediate host. |
| Progressive loss of condition with gradual paralysis. | Maedi Visna viral infection. | No cure. Slaughter all affected animals. Blood test is available. |
| Intense itch with loss of condition despite good appetite, later head raised with lip nibbling. | Scrapie due to infection by small virus like particle. | Slaughter all affected animals. |
| Fits and foaming at the mouth. | Hypomagnesaemia due to low levels of magnesium in blood stream. Common on lush pasture. | Magnesium injection given under the skin. Feed magnesium rich feed. Restrict time on lush pasture. Magnesium boluses. |
| **SUDDEN DEATH** | Anthrax ie infection with Bacillus anthracis. | Rare as source of infection is usually contaminated feed. CARE, NOTIFIABLE DISEASE AND INFECTIOUS TO PEOPLE. |
| | Any of the clostridial Diseases eg Braxy or Black Disease. | Vaccines are available and very effective. |
| | Plant poisoning eg Yew or Laurel. | Never leave hedge or tree clippings where animals can reach them. |
| | Hypomagnesaemia. See above. | Prevention can be simple and effective, see above. |
| | Lightning strike. | Post mortem should be able to show scorch marks on the skin. |

# A GUIDE TO ANIMAL AILMENTS AND TREATMENT — LAMBS

| SIGNS OF DISEASE | CAUSES | TREATMENT AND PREVENTION |
|---|---|---|
| **HEAD AND FACE.** | | |
| Nasal discharge. | Pneumonia due to virus or bacterial infection. | Antibiotic. Check environment for overcrowding and if indoors ventilation. If outdoors check shelter provision in inclement weather. |
| Nasal discharge with blood and pus. | Sheep nasal fly. Seen only in summer months. | Ivermectin may be helpful as can be or organophosphorous dips. |
| Ulcers on lips, tongue and dental pad. | Foot and Mouth Disease (unlikely to be seen only in lambs). | Check for other symptoms eg blisters on feet. If suspicious inform vet or Ministry. NOTIFIABLE DISEASE. |
| Scabs on lips, also on nostril and eyelids. | Orf ie infection by Paravaccinia virus. | Topical ointments and sprays can stop secondary bacterial infection. Isolate affected animals. Vaccine available. CARE, INFECTIOUS TO PEOPLE. |
| Scabs on face ie around eye, ears and base of horns. | Facial eczema due to bacterial infection ie Staphylococcus aureus. Head fly. | Antibiotic. Check trough space is adequate. Pour on preparations. |
| | Photosensitisation may be a factor in summer months. | Ingestion of St Johns Wort or clover may precipitate condition. Move pasture or indoors. Try steroids or antihistamines. |
| Loss of hair on face especially around eyes. | Ringworm, usually due to Trichophyton verrucosum. Rare condition. CARE, INFECTIOUS TO PEOPLE. | Topical and oral antifungal agents. |
| Salivation and drooling from the mouth. | Virus infection eg Foot and Mouth or Orf. See above. | See above for foot and Mouth and Orf. |
| | Actinobacillosis ie bacterial infection in mouth and jaw bone and elsewhere. | Antibiotic or sodium iodide intravenous weekly or potassium iodide orally daily. |
| | Colibacillosis ie Watery mouth. Due to infection by E.coli. | Antibiotic and Metoclopramide and electrolytes. Ensure good colostrum uptake. Good hygiene essential. |

| SIGNS OF DISEASE | CAUSES | TREATMENT AND PREVENTION |
| --- | --- | --- |
| **EYES** | | |
| Watery discharge from one or both eyes. | Entropion ie inturned eye lid(s). | Easily rectified by vet with minor surgery. If major problem consider breeding programme. |
| White discharge from one or both eyes sometimes with damage to the surface of the eye. | Infectious kerato-conjunctivitis due to infection by Rickettsia or Chlamydia organism. | Subconjunctival injection (job for the vet) or topical antibiotic ointment. Control is difficult/reduce crowding. |
| Discharge from one eye with or without eye damage. | Consider foreign body in the eye. | Careful search and remove and then administer antibiotic ointment. |
| Swollen eye lids. | Allergic reaction. | Antihistamines and or corticosteroids. May have to move pastures. |
| Eyes dull and lifeless. | Part of any general disease eg colisepticaemia. | Look for other symptoms and then treat generally. |
| Blindness. | Congenital cataracts. | Nothing practical can be done. |
| | Older lambs; Rape poisoning or Cerebrocortical NEcrosis. | Remove from rape field. Inject thiamine in high doses. |
| | Bracken poisoning. | Remove from source. Antibiotic and thiamine may help. |
| Yellow colour in white of the eye. | Jaundice usually the result of copper poisoning. | Oral dose of sodium sulphate may help but generally poor prognosis. |
| Membranes of the eye pale or white. | Anaemia due to worms or deficiency of iron or copper in diet. | Treat with anthelmintic. Copper given in slow release bolus. Iron by injection or orally. |
| | Rape poisoning. | Remove from offending diet. |
| Membranes of eye dark and congested. | Circulatory difficulties as part of more general disease eg pneumonia. | Check for other symptoms and treat for general disease/ see vet. |
| Eyes sunk into eye sockets. | Dehydration usually as the result of scouring. | Electrolytes as fluid replacer and treat the cause of the scour. |

| SIGNS OF DISEASE | CAUSES | TREATMENT AND PREVENTION |
|---|---|---|
| **EARS**<br>One or both ears swollen. | Abscess or blood blister. | Drain abscess and give antibiotic. Blood blister leave to reabsorb naturally. |
| One ear drooping with possible discharge from ear canal. | Bacterial infection, consider listeriosis. | Antibiotic. If listeriosis consider source of infection eg silage also practice good hygiene in lambing pen. |
| **SKIN AND FLEECE**<br>Loss of fleece with scabs and itching. | Sheep Scab due to Psoroptic mite infection. Until recently NOTIFIABLE DISEASE. Now any untreated sheep with infection may be welfare cases and farmer prosecuted. | Dip with approved sheep scab dip. CARE, ENSURE ALL SAFETY PRECAUTIONS ARE OBSERVED WHEN DIPPING. |
| Loss of fleece with itching. Parasites found. | Lice, Ticks and Keds could all be involved. | Dip or spray or pour on infected animals with recommended products. May have to be repeated every 10 to 14 days. |
| Wet staining of wool mostly around rear end with animal distressed. | Blowfly maggots. | Dag the flock ie clean and clip area of the dock. Dip or spray. Severely affected may have to be destroyed. |
| Excessively long and curly wool with nervous symptoms. | Border Disease due to virus infection in the ewe in the first 2-3 months of gestation. | None available. Separate infected and non-infected mothers. |
| Wrinkled skin with sores. | Zinc deficiency. Rare condition. | Zinc sulphate weekly. Control with zinc fertiliser on pasture. |
| **BREATHING**<br>Rapid breathing. | Pneumonia commonly due to bacterial infection eg Pasteurella. Acute infection, young animal often found dead. | Antibiotic.<br><br>Reduce stress, check ventilation if indoors. Vaccine available for Pasteurella infection. |
| | Stress due to pain, overheating or exercise. | Remove source of the stress and the symptoms should resolve quickly. |

| SIGNS OF DISEASE | CAUSES | TREATMENT AND PREVENTION |
|---|---|---|
| Shallow breathing. | Asleep or in terminal stage of illness. | No action. Check for other symptoms/ get vet. |
| Coughing. | Respiratory disease eg pneumonia due to infection. | Antibiotic, anti-inflammatory and mucolytics drugs. |
| | Unlikely to be lung worms unless in older lambs. | Anthelmintic for lung worm. See vet for diagnosis. |
| | Inhalation pneumonia following faulty drenching and dosing. | Antibiotic to control secondary infection. Improve drenching technique. |
| **TEMPERATURE** Normal range is 101.5 F - 102.5F. | | |
| Raised. | Usually means infection but may be the result of stress or pain. | Check for other symptoms. If in doubt check with vet. Antibiotic for infection. Pain killers for pain. |
| Lowered, | Check again, may be incorrect technique or reading. Hypothermia in young lambs is a common killer. May be terminally ill. | Raise body temperature with heat lamps or equivalent Warm air heaters. Check for other symptoms eg diarrhoea. |
| Shivering. | Young lambs with early stages of hypothermia. | See above. If indoors check for draughts. If outdoors, are there adequate windbreaks? |
| **DUNG** Constipation. | Can be one of the symptoms of wet mouth (more commonly diarrhoea). Not uncommon if lamb has not received colostrum. | Check for other symptoms. Liquid paraffin useful 1-2 teaspoonful. |
| Scouring. Young lambs no blood in diarrhoea. | Bacterial infection eg E. coli which also causes watery mouth symptoms. | Antibiotic and electrolytes. Keep the patient warm. Colostrum essential for prevention as is good hygiene. |
| Scouring with blood in diarrhoea. | Lambs Dysentery due to Clostridial infection. | Antibiotic and electrolytes. Keep the patient warm. antisera can be used to control outbreak. Vaccinate ewes to prevent. |

| SIGNS OF DISEASE | CAUSES | TREATMENT AND PREVENTION |
|---|---|---|
| Older lambs with diarrhoea, perhaps some blood. | Coccidiosis usually infection with Eimeria species. | Oral antibacterials eg Amprolium or sulphadimidine. Avoid overcrowding and wet areas. Prophylactic in feed medication can be used. |
| Older lambs with diarrhoea, no blood. | Parasitic Gastro-enteritis ie worms. These include Haemonchus, Ostertagia, Trichstrongylus, Oesophagostomum and Nematodiaris species. | Anthelmintic to all affected animals. Drench ewes prior to lambing and move to clean pasture ie pasture not used by sheep the previous year. |
| **BLOAT** Bloat ie abdominal distention of left side of abdomen. | Gas not being belched from rumen. Could be obstruction in gullet or failure in the mechanism to allow belching or frothy bloat where gas and fluid are mixed as a froth. Uncommon in young lambs except those bottle fed. | Stomach drench silicone or oil preparation. Get vet to check diet. |
| | Older lambs due to overeating especially lucerne or clover. | As above and restrict grazing of suspect pasture. |
| Bloat with distention on both sides of abdomen. | Severe bloat. Animal will be close to death. | May require emergency trocarisation. Get vet ASAP. |
| Swelling under belly at the navel. | Navel infection. | Antibiotic. Dip navel at birth with Iodine or spray with antibiotic. |
| | Umbilical hernia. | If small no action required. If large surgery may be needed. |
| **URINE** Urinary retention or blockage sometimes with distended abdomen. | Urolithiasis. Common in housed lambs on concentrate feed. Due to calculi(stone) blocking urethra. | Muscle relaxant drugs may help. Surgery or euthanasia for severe cases. Check diet. Salt in diet may help prevent new cases. |

| SIGNS OF DISEASE | CAUSES | TREATMENT AND PREVENTION |
|---|---|---|
| Discoloured urine often dark red in colour. | Clostridial infection. Animal usually collapsed due to toxaemia. | Antibiotic and fluid therapy. Poor prognosis. Vaccinate as prevention. |
| Pain in abdomen; seen as lying down and getting up frequently, teeth grinding and kicking while lying down. | Colic due to bloat or urolithoiasis. Clostridial infections can cause pain eg Pulpy Kidney or Lamb Dysentery. | Muscle relaxants and or pain killers plus see above. Clostridial antisera and antibiotic. Vaccinate as prevention. |

## LAMENESS

| | | |
|---|---|---|
| Feet. | Bacterial infection in the foot eg foot abscess, foot rot or foot scald. Commonly due to Fusiformis species or if abscess Corynebacteria. | Pare foot where appropriate and dress with topical spray. Inject antibiotic. Keep on dry ground and use foot baths. |
| | Virus infection eg Foot and Mouth Disease. | Check for ulcers in mouth. If in doubt call vet. NOTIFIABLE DISEASE. |
| Limbs. | Injury eg fracture, nerve damage, puncture wounds or strains. | All but most minor may need vet attention. Treat as required by symptoms. |
| | Clostridial infection eg Black Leg. | Large doses of antibiotic and antiserum. Vaccinate to prevent. |
| | Specific joint infection eg Erysipelas or C. Pyogenes. | Antibiotic and good hygiene required. Clean pens and dips. Dip navels at birth. |
| | Tick Pyaemia due to Staph. aureus abscesses in the joints and may be elsewhere. | Antibiotic. Tick control can help. |
| Deformed limbs. | Rickets due to a dietary imbalance of calcium/phosphorus and Vit D. | Oral or injectable calcium/phosphorous and Vit D preparations. Check and maintain adequate diet. |
| Stiff limbs. | Vitamin E/ Selenium deficiency. | Vit E and selenium injections. Nutritional supplements. |

| SIGNS OF DISEASE | CAUSES | TREATMENT AND PREVENTION |
|---|---|---|
| **BEHAVIOUR** | | |
| Loss of appetite. | Any infection causing a rise in temperature. | Check for other symptoms before starting treatment. |
| | Pain; check mouth for sores; check for abdominal pain. Pain causing lameness unlikely to cause loss of appetite. | Treatment depends on cause of pain. Pain killers, anti-inflammatory drugs and antibiotic may all be helpful. |
| Dull and weak with low rectal temperature. | Hypothermia due to inadequate shelter or lack of food or both. | Warm gently. Feed with stomach tube if not sucking/Intra Peritomeal glucose injection. Ensure adequate shelter for ewes and lambs. Make sure lamb gets enough colostrum. |
| Nervous Signs eg twisted head and neck 'star gazing'. | Daft Lamb Disease ie congenital disease of Border Leicester sheep. | No treatment. Review breeding programme. |
| Lambs born weak with tremors and wool abnormalities. | Border Disease due to viral infection. | No treatment. Isolate all infected ewes from unaffected. |
| Blindness and walking in circles. | Cerebrocortical Necrosis due to thiamine deficiency. | High levels of thiamine by injection. |
| Walking in circles and head pressing. | Middle ear infection or Listeriosis. | Antibiotic. Avoid silage feeding. Good hygiene important. |
| | Gid (Sturdy) ie tape worm cyst in brain. | Surgery to remove cyst. Routine tape worm dosing of all dogs. |
| Head pressing with peculiar gait, then recumbency. | Louping Ill due to virus infection. | Antisera may be some use if used early. Vaccine available. Control tick which is the intermediate host. |
| Uncoordinated limb movements and swaying. | Swayback. Due to a congenital copper deficiency. | Nothing much helps to treat clinical cases. Control by giving pregnant ewes copper injections or slow release copper bolus. |

45

| SIGNS OF DISEASE | CAUSES | TREATMENT AND PREVENTION |
|---|---|---|
| **SUDDEN DEATH** | Anthrax ie infection with Bacillus anthracis. | Rare, as source of infection is usually contaminated feed. NOTIFIABLE DISEASE AND INFECTIOUS TO PEOPLE. |
| | Any of the Clostridial Diseases eg Lamb Dysentery or Pulpy Kidney. | Vaccines are available and very effective. |
| | Plant poisoning eg Yew or Laurel. | Never leave hedge or tree clippings where animals can reach them. |
| | Lightning Strike. | Post mortem should be able to show scorch marks on skin. |

# PIGS

Pigs when kept as individuals and not in groups will quickly assume an individual personality, where it can be seen that they are the most intelligent of all the farm animals. They are also, given a chance, the cleanest of animals and will not willingly soil their living quarters.

Kept in groups they can be subject to the most appalling antisocial behaviour such as bullying, tail and ear biting (or any other appendage that comes easily to the mouth) and infanticide. This trait can be alleviated almost entirely by keeping pigs with a high regard to their welfare. Making sure that they are warm, well housed and not overcrowded does not mean antisocial behaviour will be eliminated but it will help a very great deal. Pigs kept in groups can also be subject to severe epidemics of a variety of illnesses which can spell the death knell to any enterprise.

There is a good range of vaccines against many pig diseases which can be very useful in the right circumstances, but despite the risks the only vaccination which is a must for any pig kept for breeding purposes is against Erysipelas (a soil saprophyte). It is a disease which can strike at any time and create havoc.

It may also be worthwhile to inject against Parvo virus disease which can be a scourge in a breeding unit, causing a wide range of infertility problems. Do not inject against Parvo and not Erysipelas.

# A GUIDE TO ANIMAL AILMENTS AND TREATMENT — PIGS

| SIGNS OF DISEASE | CAUSES | TREATMENT AND PREVENTION |
|---|---|---|
| **HEAD AND FACE** Discharge from the eyes. | Slight discharge not uncommon in short nosed breeds. | No action. |
| | Dusty environment causing irritation to eye membranes. | Improve ventilation and change bedding. |
| | Conjunctivitis due to bacterial infection; often sequel to bad ventilation. | Antibiotic eye ointment or drops. |
| | Rhinitis unlikely cause in adults as affected pigs not used for breeding. | Any clinically affected animals cull from herd. |
| Eyes dull and lifeless. | Part of any general disease. | Check for other symptoms before attempting diagnosis or treatment. |
| Membranes of the eye pale or white. | Anaemia due to internal parasites (gut or stomach worms), or internal haemorrhage caused by eg stomach ulcers. | Dose with anthelmintic. Difficult to treat, supportive treatment only. |
| Membranes of the eye yellow. | Jaundice usually the result of bacterial infection eg Leptospira or fungus eg Aspergillus. | Antibiotic. Check water supply for cleanliness. Rodent control. Feed likely source of fungus/ check. |
| Eyes sunk into sockets. | Dehydration usually as the result of vomiting and or scouring. | Electrolytes as fluid replacement. Other treatment may be indicated when a diagnosis is made. |
| Nasal discharge with sneezing. | Dusty environment. | Improve ventilation and get rid of dust. |
| | Atrophic Rhinitis or Inclusion Body Rhinitis is a disease of young pigs. | Any adult animals with twisted snouts should be culled from the herd and not bred from. |
| | Upper respiratory infection by virus or bacteria. | Antibiotic may be required for treatment. |

| SIGNS OF DISEASE | CAUSES | TREATMENT AND PREVENTION |
|---|---|---|
| Salivation. | Sores in mouth or on tongue due to bacterial infection following an injury or bad tooth. Possible tumour (rare). | Further investigation may be needed. Treat with antibiotic. Euthanasia on welfare grounds. |
| Salivation with sores in mouth and on snout. | Consider possibility of Foot and Mouth Disease or Swine Vesicular Disease. Both are virus diseases and NOTIFIABLE DISEASES. | If there is any suspicion of either these two diseases you must get veterinary advice or notify the local Divisional Veterinary Officer ASAP. |
| Itching and skin thickening around and between the eyes. | Mange due to infection by a mite Sarcoptes scabiei. | Topical or injectable ectoparasiticides. |

**EARS**

| | | |
|---|---|---|
| One or both ears swollen. | Common cause is abscess or haematoma (blood blister). | Lance and drain abscess. Leave haematoma alone if possible as blood will be absorbed over a few weeks. In both cases it will be better to isolate the patient over the acute period. |
| Brown discharge from one or both ears with some irritation. | Mange due to Sarcoptes scabiei. Common. | As above, topical ectoparasites or injectable ivermectin. |
| Red discolouration of both ears. | If healthy, outdoor pig, sunburn. | Provide shade and wallow. |
| Blue or purple discolouration of both ears. | Terminal stage of many different diseases eg Blue Ear Disease or Salmonella etc. | Pig is acutely ill. Get vet ASAP. |
| | Heart failure. | Poor prognosis. Needs vet attention. |

**SKIN**

| | | |
|---|---|---|
| Skin itchy with brown discharge on back around eyes and ears and on legs. | Mange due to Sarcoptes scabiei. | As above, treat with topical eg Porect or injectable eg Ivermectin, ectoparasiticide. Treat and move to clean accommodation. Eradicate by treating every 10 days. |

| SIGNS OF DISEASE | CAUSES | TREATMENT AND PREVENTION |
|---|---|---|
| Skin itching without discharge. | Check for lice (Haematopinus suis). | Topical or injectable ectoparasiticide. |
| Skin with generalised redness especially the ears. | If otherwise healthy and outdoors, this is sunburn. | Provide shade and mud wallows. |
| Skin with red raised sores, usually diamond shape along back. | Swine Erysipelas chronic form of infection by Erysipelothrix insodiosa. | Penicillin is still the most effective treatment. Vaccination is highly effective. |
| Skin with purple discolouration of ears and belly. | May be the terminal sign of any toxic or septicaemic disease but considering particular Salmonella or if just farrowed acute metritis. | Get vet ASAP. Will need to check for other symptoms to make a diagnosis before treatment is started. |

**BREATHING**
Normal respiratory rate is 12-15 per minute.

| | | |
|---|---|---|
| Rapid breathing. | Stress due to pain or hyperthermia or over exercise. | Identify and remove source of stress. If hyperthermic douse with cold water. Sedatives may be useful. |
| | Pneumonia due to virus, bacteria of lungworm (Metastrongylus apri) infection. Swine flu is common virus infection, Pasteurella and Haemophilus are common bacterial infections. | Antibiotic by injection or in feed or in water. Anthelmintic for lungworm. Get vet to check diagnosis and environment for adequate ventilation. |
| | Consider chronic heart failure if pig is old and overweight. | Difficult to treat and poor prognosis. Vet may try cardiac and respiratory stimulants and diuretics if there is fluid retention. |

| SIGNS OF DISEASE | CAUSES | TREATMENT AND PREVENTION |
|---|---|---|
| Shallow breathing. | Probably asleep. | No action/ let sleeping pigs lie! |
| | Possible in terminal stage of illness but there would be other symptoms. | Check for other symptoms. |
| | Some pigs with high temperatures eg with Erysipelas will lie very still. | Check temperature before treating. If in doubt get the vet. |
| Coughing. | Respiratory disease/ see above for pneumonia. | See above. |
| Sporadic dry cough in outdoor pigs. | Likely cause is lungworm or migrating roundworm. | Oral or injectable anthelmintic. Move to clean pasture. Pasture may need resting or cultivating for some years to be rid of the parasite. |
| Lowered temperature. | Check again, may be incorrect technique. If temperature is 2-3 degrees lower than normal, the pig may be terminally ill. | Check again for other symptoms. If in doubt get the vet. |
| Sweating. | Pigs do not appear to sweat. | Pigs if too hot will lose heat through the skin. They also pant and use any source of water and mud to cool off. |
| Shivering. | See above for lowered temperature but probably not serious. | Thin sows often shiver to raise body temperature as they have difficulty in keeping warm in cold weather if building is not weatherproof and not insulated. |
| **DUNG** Constipation. | Quite common in sows before and after farrowing. | Liquid paraffin in the food or drinking water. Bran either in feed or as a mash. Vegetables and grass can be useful. |
| Scouring, without blood. | Some virus infections common eg Epidemic diarrhoea and T.G.E. | No vaccine available. Most adults will self-cure. Make sure they have plentiful access to fresh drinking water. |
| | Parasitism due to bowel worms eg Strongyles or whipworms. | Regular worming with anthelmintic and good hygiene. |

| SIGNS OF DISEASE | CAUSES | TREATMENT AND PREVENTION |
|---|---|---|
| Scouring, with blood. | Bacterial infection eg Salmonella (CARE, COULD BE INFECTIOUS TO PEOPLE) or Swine Dysentery at times of stress eg farrowing. | Salmonella is a NOTIFIABLE DISEASE. Antibiotic treatment and hygiene is vital. Tiamutin and Lincocin are drugs of choice for treatment of Dysentery. |
| Vomiting. | Gastritis as the result of overeating or eating something unsuitable or stomach worms or stress resulting in ulceration of the stomach wall. | Remove unsuitable diet and give fluids only for 24-36 hours. If suspect stomach worms dose with anthelmintic. |
|  | Virus infections eg Epidemic Diarrhoea or T.G.E. | Adult pigs will self-cure providing they have plenty to drink. |
| Abdominal distension without pain. | Ascites ie Dropsy as the result of heart or liver failure. | Difficult to treat poor prognosis. Diuretics may be helpful. |
|  | Peritonitis usually as a result of stomach or bowel ulceration. | Difficult to treat. Antibiotic may be helpful if early in disease. |
|  | Abdominal tumour. | Euthanasia on welfare grounds. |
| Abdominal distension with pain. | Stomach or intestinal torsion. | Euthanasia on welfare grounds. |
|  | Outdoor pigs might have a fluke infection. | Fluke Anthelmintic and avoid ill drained pasture where the snail is the intermediate host for the parasite. |
| Abdominal distension with blood or pus in urine. | Cystitis and pus in the kidneys (Pyelonephritis) Can be painful although abdominal distension may not be too apparent. | Antibiotic, particularly in early stages. May be necessary to cull chronic cases. |

| SIGNS OF DISEASE | CAUSES | TREATMENT AND PREVENTION |
|---|---|---|
| **INFERTILITY**<br>FEMALE<br>Failure to come into season. | Hormone imbalance or failure. These may be inherited or due to faulty nutrition or management. | Hormone therapy may be helpful. Check diet sow may be too thin or too fat. Keep animal within sound sight and smell of boar. |
| | May be pregnant. | Check. |
| | Vitamin deficiency eg Vit A or Biotin. | Feed analysis may be useful to check for deficiency. Inclusion of vitamin supplements in the ration. |
| | Failure to notice when in season. Heat period in the winter may be short. | Improve management. |
| Irregular heat periods. Normal cycle is every 21 days. | Cystic ovaries due to hormone imbalance. | Hormone injections may be helpful. |
| | Infectious infertility/virus eg Smedi/Parvo/ bacterial disease eg Erysipelas, Leptospirosis. | Needs careful investigation by vet. Blood tests and swabs most helpful. Depending on cause, vaccines and antibiotic may be used to treat. Management also has large contribution to make. |
| **ABORTION** | General virus disease with other symptoms eg Swine Fever, Aujesky's Disease or Blue Ear Disease. | Blood tests required for diagnosis. Swine Fever and Aujesky's are Notifiable Disease. Blue Ear was notifiable until recently. No treatment available. |
| | Specific virus diseases eg Parvo virus or Smedi infections. | Vaccine available for Parvo infections not for Smedi. Try to infect susceptible stock before pregnancy. |
| | Bacterial infection eg Swine Erysipelas and Leptospirosis. CARE, INFECTIOUS TO PEOPLE. | Vaccine a must against Erysipelas. Antibiotic, hygiene and rodent control used against Leptospirosis. |
| Vaginal discharge. Clear discharge with or without blood stain. | If pregnant, may be about to give birth. Slight discharge may be apparent when in season. | Get experienced help to check if in doubt. If in season there should be other behavioural signs. |

| SIGNS OF DISEASE | CAUSES | TREATMENT AND PREVENTION |
|---|---|---|
| Purulent smelly discharge sometimes with straining after farrowing. | Metritis ie infection in the genital tract with or without retained piglets or afterbirth. | Check for piglets and afterbirth and remove where possible. Antibiotic by injection and in pessaries or irrigation. Job for the vet. |
| Discharge without straining after farrowing. | Farrowing Fever syndrome ie after farrowing when the udder is inflamed and little or no milk is produced. | Antibiotic, corticosteroids and oxytocin. May be helpful. Make sure that sow is not over fed and constipated before farrowing. |
| | Specific infection eg Blue Ear Disease. | No specific treatment. |

**INFERTILITY**
MALE

| | | |
|---|---|---|
| | Deficiency diseases eg Vit A causes lack of libido. | Either Vit A injections or nutritional supplement. |
| | Orthopaedic problems eg sore back, legs or pelvis. | Get vet to check and treat any lameness. |

**MASTITIS**
All glands

| | | |
|---|---|---|
| affected, red, sore and painful. | Acute bacterial infection causing metritis. | Antibiotic, corticosteriods and oxytocin. Improve hygiene, clip piglets teeth. Vaccination may be helpful in some cases. |
| Less acute syndrome with vaginal discharge and failure to let down milk. | Farrowing fever due to a variety of bacterial infections. Constipation may be a factor in the syndrome. | Antibiotic, etc as for mastitis. Massage the udder with udder cream. Prevent constipation by cutting down on feed prior to farrowing and make up balance with bran or give liquid paraffin. |
| Lack of milk after farrowing without animal being ill. | Lack of mammary development in immature gilts. | Milk may come after a few hours. |
| | Premature farrowing. | Milk may come after a few hours. |
| | Failure of milk let down. | Oxytocin injection will bring almost immediate results. |
| Only one or two glands swollen and sore. | Mastitis see above. | Treat as for generalised mastitis. If animal has glands that are still hard and swollen after piglets are weaned then cull the sow. |

| SIGNS OF DISEASE | CAUSES | TREATMENT AND PREVENTION |
|---|---|---|

## LAMENESS

### Feet

| SIGNS OF DISEASE | CAUSES | TREATMENT AND PREVENTION |
|---|---|---|
| Swelling around the base of one or more claw. | Septic joints in the feet. Common. Many due to poor flooring causing damage to the sole allowing infection to penetrate. Biotin deficiency may also predispose to foot infections. | Antibiotic must be given as soon as lesions are seen. Chronic abscesses may require surgery. Get vet to check flooring. Biotin supplement in the feed. |
| Blisters around and between base of claws. | Virus infection cause blisters and lameness ie Foot and Mouth and Swine Vesicular Disease. Both are rare in the UK and both are NOTIFIABLE DISEASES. | Check for blisters in mouth and snout and if suspicious contact your vet or Divisional Veterinary Officer ASAP. |
| General foot soreness without obvious lesions. | Laminitis ie inflammation in the foot due to overfeeding or toxaemia after farrowing. | Pain killers and antibiotic if appropriate. Reduce feed and add more roughage. |

### Limbs

| SIGNS OF DISEASE | CAUSES | TREATMENT AND PREVENTION |
|---|---|---|
| | Injury eg fracture, nerve damage, puncture wounds and strains. | All but the most minor will need some veterinary attention. |
| Swollen, painful joints. | Non-septic arthritis caused by trauma to the joint. | Pain killing, corticosteroids and non-steroidal anti-inflammatory drugs can all be used. Animal may have to be culled. |
| | Swine Erysipelas can cause non-septic arthritis. | Treat early in the disease to prevent arthritis. Once arthritis is present antibiotic may have little value. All adult animals **must** be vaccinated twice a year. |
| | Septic arthritis ie pus in the joint(s). Due to a variety of bacteria. | Early treatment with an antibiotic that can cross the joint membrane barrier is vital. eg Ampicillin. Prognosis is poor. |

| SIGNS OF DISEASE | CAUSES | TREATMENT AND PREVENTION |
|---|---|---|
| Hind leg paralysis ie unable to stand. | Usually some form of pelvic or spinal injury. often before or after farrowing. | Pain killing drugs corticosteroids and non-steroidal anti-inflammatory drugs may all be helpful. Soft deep bedding and good nursing. If no response in a few days, euthanasia on welfare grounds. |
| | Spinal abscess often after tail biting. | No treatment. Euthanasia on welfare grounds. |
| **BEHAVIOUR** Loss of appetite. | Any fever or pain especially if abdominal. | Check for other symptoms. |
| Vomiting. | See above - after diarrhoea. | See above. |
| **NERVOUS SIGNS** Head tilt to left or right side with circling to the tilted side. | Middle ear infection due to a variety of possible bacterial infections. | Early treatment with appropriate antibiotic. General nursing care. |
| Above symptoms with head pressing and salivation. | Meningitis eg listeriosis bacterial infection. | Early treatment with antibiotic. Check feed for possible source of infection. |
| Above symptoms followed by collapse and convulsions. | Consider salt poisoning ie water deprivation. | Remove feed and make sure animal can drink small amount regularly. Make sure all livestock have access at all times to clean fresh water. |
| Muscles tremors followed by stiffness, rigidity and convulsions. | Tetanus (lockjaw) due to infection into a small wound which may or may not be found. | Antibiotic, antitoxin and sedatives. Good hygiene to prevent. Can also use vaccine on problem farms. |
| **PROLAPSES** Rectum. | Common in heavy pregnant sows. | Can be replaced with vet attention. Cull after pigs are weaned. |
| Rectum and or vagina. | Common in heavy pregnant sows. | Can be replaced and repaired with vet attention. Cull after pigs are weaned. |
| Uterine prolapse after farrowing. | Prolonged straining after farrowing is finished. | Acute vet emergency. Very difficult to treat and animal may die or have to be euthanased on welfare grounds. |

| SIGNS OF DISEASE | CAUSES | TREATMENT AND PREVENTION |
|---|---|---|
| **THIN SOW SYNDROME** | Insufficient feed. Worms eg gut or stomach worms. Poor housing causing draughts and wet bedding. | Improve feed, treat animals with anthelmintic, improve insulation within quarters and stop draughts. |
| **VICES** Bullying and fighting. | Poor husbandry. | Ensure adequate feed and trough space. Individual feeders good idea. Allow access to plenty of straw if in yards. Find the chief culprit and isolate. |
| If outdoors, excessive digging. | Natural habit. | Can be curbed by fitting nose rings. |
| **SUDDEN DEATH** ie without prior symptoms. | | |
| Anthrax. | Infection by Bacillus anthracis. Disease is NOTIFIABLE when diagnosed in the dead animal. CARE, INFECTIOUS TO PEOPLE. | All sudden deaths should be notified to the vet or to the Ministry. Vaccine is available. Disinfection is very important in limiting outbreak. |
| Erysipelas. | Acute bacterial infection. | All adult pigs should be vaccinated. |
| Swine Fever. | Virus infection. NOTIFIABLE in the UK. | Rare, not in the UK at the moment. |
| Electrocution. | Faulty wiring. | Extreme care required on investigation. If at all in doubt turn off electricity at mains and get qualified electrician. |
| Heart failure. | Old heavy sows may be more prone to die in this way. Erysipelas may be a factor in damaging the heart valves. | Cull sows before they get too old and fat. |

# A GUIDE TO ANIMAL AILMENTS AND TREATMENT — PIGLETS, WEANERS AND FATTENERS

| SIGNS OF DISEASE | CAUSES | TREATMENT AND PREVENTION |
|---|---|---|
| **HEAD AND FACE** Discharge from eyes. | Dusty environment causing irritation to eye membranes. | Improve ventilation and change bedding. |
| | Conjunctivitis due to bacterial infection. | Antibiotic eye cream. |
| | Rhinitis either Inclusion body rhinitis (herpes virus) or Atrophic (various bacterial agents). | Antibacterial, injectable and oral as treatment and control. Vaccine available for Atrophic control. Improve ventilation and hygiene. |
| Eyes dull and lifeless. | Part of any general disease or hypoglycaemia. | Check for other symptoms and treat accordingly. |
| Blindness. | Congenital defect causing eye malformations. | Nothing can be done. Check breeding policy. |
| Membranes of eye pale or white. | Anaemia iron deficiency. | All young pigs need iron injection in the first few days of life or oral iron until they are weaned to avoid anaemia. |
| Eyes sunk into sockets. | Dehydration as the result of scouring. | Electrolytes as fluid replacement. Scour may require antibiotic if infection is present. |
| Nasal discharge with sneezing. | Dusty environment. | Improve ventilation. Get rid of dust. |
| | Atrophic or Inclusion Body Rhinitis (see above). | Antibiotics can be used to treat but must be used early in life (from a few days old) to be successful. Vaccine available for Atrophic Rhinitis. Improve ventilation and hygiene. |
| Twisted nostril to left or right, sometimes with difficulty in breathing. | Either type of Rhinitis. See above. | See above and remember to buy in pigs from rhinitis free sources. |

| SIGNS OF DISEASE | CAUSES | TREATMENT AND PREVENTION |
|---|---|---|
| Short snout; apart from what you would expect from breed. | May be Rhinitis but more likely if only a few involved to be congenital malformation. | If congenital nothing can be done. |
| Domed head. | Hydrocephalus. | Euthanasia on welfare grounds. |
| Salivation with sores in mouth and on snout. | Bacterial infection following an injury or virus infection eg Foot and Mouth Disease or Swine Vesicular Disease (both NOTIFIABLE DISEASES). | Antibiotic get vet to check as if suspect viral cause need to notify authorities ASAP. |
| Scabs and sores around face and cheeks. | Facial eczema/ bacterial infection due to piglets fighting for a place at the udder. | Antibiotic and clip youngsters teeth. |
| Inability to suckle. | Cleft palate. | Euthanasia on welfare ground. |
| **EARS**<br>One or both ears swollen. | Common cause is haematoma (blood blister). Less likely, abscess. | Better to leave haematoma if possible but if causing distress lance and then isolate the pig. Abscesses must be lanced and drained and patient given antibiotic. |
| Brown discharge from one or both ears with some irritation. | Mange due to Sarcoptes scabiei. Unlikely in very young pigs. | Topical ectoparasiticides or injectable Ivermectin. |
| **SKIN**<br>Absence of skin over an area at birth. | Inherited condition. | No treatment. May have to change breeding programme. |
| Skin covered with crusty brown discharge non-itchy. | Greasy Pig Disease, usually pigs over three weeks old. Staph. hyicus infection. | Early treatment with antibiotic. Clean and disinfect accommodation. Clip youngsters teeth. |
| Skin with brown discharge on back around eyes and ears. Itchy. | Mange due to mite Sarcoptes scabiei. | Topical (eg Porect) or injectable (ivermectin) ectoparasiticdes. Treat sows before farrowing and move to clean accommodation. Eradicate by treating all pigs every ten days. |

| SIGNS OF DISEASE | CAUSES | TREATMENT AND PREVENTION |
|---|---|---|
| Skin itching without discharge. | Check for lice. Haematopinus suis. | Topical or injectable ectopraristes (see above). |
| Skin with round raised areas of reddened skin. | Pityriasis Rosea, cause unknown. | Will self-cure. |
| | Ringworm (much less common) CARE, INFECTIOUS TO PEOPLE. | Oral antifungal agent eg Griseofulvin or topical eg Natamycin. Treatment and prevention. |
| Skin covered in small red sores that turn scabby. | Pig Pox, due to a virus. | None required, will self-cure. |
| Skin with red raised sores (diamond shaped) along back mainly. | Swine Erysipel as (chronic infection) NOT in piglets usually seen for first time in fatteners. | Penicillin is highly effective. Effective vaccine is available. |
| Skin with blood blotches just under the skin in piglets just a few days old. | Haemolytic Disease of the new born, piglets often found dead. | Transfer remaining litter to other sow in milk or use milk substitute. Change the boar if a regular problem, cull the sow. |
| Skin with generalised redness, especially the ears. | If pigs are outdoors, this is sunburn. | Provide shade and mud wallows. |
| Skin thickening with grey discolouration, non itchy. | Parakeratosis ie Zinc deficiency. Pigs usually 2-4 months old. | Zinc supplement in the diet. |
| Skin with purple discolouration of ears and belly. | Any septicaemia can cause these symptoms but consider in particular Salmonella and Swine Fever. | Get vet ASAP will need to look for other symptoms to make a diagnosis before treatment. CARE, Salmonella COULD AFFECT PEOPLE. Swine Fever is a NOTIFIABLE DISEASE. |

| SIGNS OF DISEASE | CAUSES | TREATMENT AND PREVENTION |
|---|---|---|
| **BREATHING** | | |
| Rapid breathing. | Stress due to pain or overheating (hyperthermia) or exercise. | Identify and remove source of stress. If hyperthermic apply cold water. |
| | Pneumonia due to virus, bacteria or lungworms. | Antibiotic, by injection or in feed or water. Anthelmintic for lungworm. Get vet to check environment as well as treat animal. |
| Shallow breathing. | Probably asleep or possibly in terminal stage of illness. | No action. Check for other symptoms. |
| Coughing. | Respiratory Disease eg pneumonia. | See above. |
| | Young pigs consider Barker Syndrome due to recessive gene. | Check breeding programme. |
| | Outdoor pigs consider lung worm. | Anthelmintic either oral or injectable. Move to clean pasture. |
| **TEMPERATURE** Normal range is 101.5-102.5 F | | |
| Raised. | Often as the result of infection by bacteria or virus. | Further investigation required before treatment with antibiotic. |
| | Pigs are very susceptible to hyperthermia in hot weather. | Apply cold water. Sedative may be useful. |
| | Pain and stress can often cause a mild fever. | Identify source of stress analgesics for pain. |
| Lowered. | Check again, may be incorrect technique. Baby pigs are very susceptible to low environmental temperatures if not feeding properly. | Raise temperatures with artificial heat (80-90F) If sow has no milk foster piglets or give milk substitute or glucose and fluids. |
| | May be terminally ill. | Check for other symptoms. |

| SIGNS OF DISEASE | CAUSES | TREATMENT AND PREVENTION |
|---|---|---|
| Sweating. | Pigs do not appear to sweat. | Pigs if too hot lose heat through the skin. They also pant and use any source of water and mud to cool off. |
| Shivering. | See above for lowered temperature. | Pigs shiver to raise body temperature and also huddle together for warmth. |
| **DUNG** Constipation. | Not common in young pigs but may be a secondary to Bowel Oedema. | Liquid paraffin or Epsom Salts in drinking water or bran in the feed. |
| Scouring. Neonatal Pigs. | Bacterial infection eg E. coli, Clostridium or Campylobacter species. | Antibiotic, electrolytes, good nursing care. Vaccine can be helpful. Hygiene very important. |
| | Virus infection eg T.G.E or Rotavirus. | General nursing care and electrolytes. |
| Age 1-3 weeks. | As above with the addition of Coccidiosis. | Teat affected with coccidiostat plus electrolytes. Prevent with good hygiene and treating sows with coccidiostat in feed prior to farrowing. |
| Post weaning. | Bacterial infection eg E. coli and Salmonella. Viral infection eg T.G.E., Epidemic Diarrhoea. Worms eg ascaris or more likely Strongyloides, Oesophagostomum or Trichuris. | Antibiotic in feed or preferably in drinking water. Good nursing care and electrolytes. Strict hygiene is essential and avoid stress. Anthelmintic and dose sows before farrowing to prevent infection in the litter. |
| Scouring with blood in the diarrhoea. Neonatal pigs. | Clostridial infection. Diarrhoea is often white with blood splashes. | Antibiotic can help but antisera may be more useful. Vaccinate sows to protect the piglets. |
| | Campylobacter enteritis (Vibrio). | Antibiotic eg Tylosin and Tiamutin may be most effective. |
| Age 1-3 weeks. | See above plus Coccidiosis. | As with all other types of scour with blood, vet needs to make diagnosis before treatment begins. |

| SIGNS OF DISEASE | CAUSES | TREATMENT AND PREVENTION |
|---|---|---|
| Post weaning. | As above for younger pigs plus Swine Dysentery due to a spirochaete infection. Porcine Intestinal Adenomatosis (PIA) due to Campylobacter infection. | Lincocin, Tiamutin and Dimetridazole are drugs of choice in treatment. Good hygiene is essential. Tylosin is often drug of choice. |
| Vomiting. | Young pigs, Vomiting and Wasting Disease due to a Coronavirus. | No treatment. Try and expose sows and gilts to infection before farrowing. |
| | Other infections eg TGE can cause vomiting but usually with diarrhoea. | Check diagnosis. |
| Abdominal distention. | Gradual swelling of abdomen due to imperforate anus. | Surgery rarely effective. Euthanase on welfare grounds. Do not breed from that sow again. |
| | Peritonitis rare. | Treatment unlikely to be effective. |
| | Intestinal torsion. | Pigs, usually weaners and older commonly found dead or dying. |
| **LAMENESS** Feet. | Foot lesions in sucking pigs due mostly to poor flooring can lead to septic joints in the foot. | Antibiotic can help but improve the flooring. |
| | Foot Rot is bacterial infection following damage to the foot. | Early treatment with antibiotic. |
| | Foot and Mouth Disease and Swine Vesicular Disease. Both are rare in UK and both are NOTIFIABLE DISEASES. | Contact your vet or Ministry vet ASAP if suspicious. |

| SIGNS OF DISEASE | CAUSES | TREATMENT AND PREVENTION |
|---|---|---|
| Limbs. | Injury eg fracture, nerve damage puncture wounds and strain. | All but most minor will need some vet attention. |
| | Joint Ill ie infection in the joints. | Antibiotic as early as possible. |
| | Arthritis in fattening pigs due to Mycoplasma infection. | Antibiotic as early as possible (Lincocin often drug of choice.) |
| | Splay leg congenital defect. | Do not breed affected pigs. Attention to flooring. |
| | Deficiency Disease eg Osteomalacia/Rickets due to calcium Vit D deficiency. | Calcium and Vit D supplements. Check diet for calcium phosphorus and Vit D ratios. |
| | Osteochondrosis and Osteoarthritis due to rapid early growth. | Steroids/ aspirin may help. Nursing and soft bedding. |
| Hind leg paralysis. | Injury. | Pain killers and soft bedding. If no response within a few days euthanase on welfare grounds. |
| | Spinal abscess often after tail biting. | No treatment. |
| **BEHAVIOUR** Loss of appetite. | Any fever or pain especially if abdominal. | Check for other symptoms. |
| | Hypoglycaemia in youngsters due to lack of milk. | Fluids, glucose and warmth. |
| **NERVOUS SIGNS** Mild tremors when standing, gone when asleep. | Congenital tremors, six types recognised. Some due to congenital disorders, some due to virus infection. | Need further investigation. If due to virus may be Swine Fever and is NOTIFIABLE DISEASE. If not may require changes to breeding programme. |
| Convulsions after head pressing and circling. | Salt poisoning or water deprivation. | Remove feed and allow controlled access to water. Ensure access to clean water at all times. |

| SIGNS OF DISEASE | CAUSES | TREATMENT AND PREVENTION |
|---|---|---|
| Unco-orindation and loss of balance, squeaky voice, puffy eye lids, lateral recumbency and paddling of feet. | Bowel oedema as the result of an entero toxaemia from E.coli. | Antibiotic corticosteroid. Avoid stress at weaning time and do not over feed at weaning. |
| Uncoordination and convulsions with high temperature. | Streptococcal meningitis. Common in weaned pigs. | Antibiotic eg ampicillin or penicillin most useful for treatment. In feed or in water antibiotic useful as prevention. |
| Muscle stiffness, stiff gait followed by convulsions. | Tetanus due to infection by Clostridium tetani into a wound. | Antibiotic, antiser and sedation. Good hygiene to prevent. Can also use vaccine on problem farms. |

### BLEEDING DISORDERS

| | | |
|---|---|---|
| Bleeding from navel. | Unknown. Occurs shortly after birth. | Ligate or clamp navel at birth. Vit K injections or supplements may be helpful. |
| Signs of bleeding in the skin and throughout the body. | Haemolytic disease of the new born. See above. | Transfer litters to other sows or use milk substitutes. Use different boar if a herd problem, cull the sow. |

### VICES

| | | |
|---|---|---|
| Tail, Ear and Flank Biting. | Poor husbandry. | Ensure adequate feed and trough space. Check ventilation. Allow access to plenty of straw. Find the chief culprit and isolate and reduce stocking density. |

### SUDDEN DEATH

| | | |
|---|---|---|
| ie without prior symptoms | Anthrax ie infection by Bacillus anthracis. Disease is Notifiable when animal is dead. CARE, INFECTIOUS TO PEOPLE. | All sudden deaths should be notified to vet or Ministry. Vaccine available. Disinfection is very important in limiting outbreak. |
| Bacterial infection. | Swine Erysipelas. | Vaccine available. |

| SIGNS OF DISEASE | CAUSES | TREATMENT AND PREVENTION |
|---|---|---|
| Virus infection. | Swine Fever. NOTIFIABLE DISEASE. | Not in UK at present. |
| Electrocution. | Faulty wiring. | Extreme care required on investigation. If in doubt at all get qualified electrician. |
| Stress Syndrome. | Stress precipitates onset in pigs with genetic defect. | Avoid stressing pigs at all times eg do not feed fat pigs prior to loading. Breed out defect. |
| Slurry poisoning. | Gases given off by slurry, without adequate ventilation can be poisonous. | Care required on investigation. Improve ventilation. |

# GOATS

Goats are perhaps the most engaging of all agricultural animals and were arguably the first species to be domesticated by man. They have become increasingly prominent on the domestic British scene over the last twenty years with the upsurge in interest in fibre production for mohair and cashmere.

Goats are hardy creatures, willing to survive in conditions that no self respecting sheep would tolerate for long, but have a low pain threshold and make very poor patients.

Like sheep, they can die very readily and do need vaccinating against the Clostridial diseases especially Enterotoxaemia.

It is common to put goats and sheep together as a group as far as disease treatment and prevention is concerned. There are many similarities but there are almost as many differences and goats must be seen and treated as the different species they are.

A milker can produce her own body weight in milk in 10–12 days and requires very careful management at this time.

# A GUIDE TO ANIMAL AILMENTS AND TREATMENT — GOATS

| SIGNS OF DISEASE | CAUSES | TREATMENT AND PREVENTION |
|---|---|---|
| **HEAD AND FACE** | | |
| Nasal Discharge | Pneumonia due to virus or bacterial infection. Most common infection is due to Pasteurella species. | Antibiotic for most cases. If animal is kept indoors check ventilation. Vaccine available for Pasteurella control. |
| | Bacterial or fungal infection in upper respiratory tract. | Antibiotic or antifungal preparations after swabbing to make diagnosis. |
| Ulcers on lips, tongue and dental pad. | Foot and Mouth Disease. Now rare. | Check for other symptoms eg blisters around feet. If suspicious inform vet or Ministry. NOTIFIABLE DISEASE. |
| Scabs on lips also on nostrils and eye lids. | Orf, ie infection by Paravaccinia virus. | Topical ointments and sprays can stop secondary bacterial infection. Isolate affected animals. Vaccine available. |
| Scabs on face ie around eye, ears and base of horn. | Facial eczema due to bacterial infection ie Staphylococcus aureus. Not common but may be complicated by fly worry. | Antibiotic and check to make sure trough space is adequate. Insecticides can be used and head protected by head cap. |
| Loss of hair on face especially around the eyes. | Ringworm, usually due to Trichophyton verrucosum. Rare condition but more common than in sheep. CARE, INFECTIOUS TO PEOPLE. | Topical and oral antifungal agents. Do not feed Griseofulvin to pregnant animals. |
| Salivation and drooling from the mouth. | Viral infection eg Orf or Foot and Mouth. See Above. | See above. |
| | Actinobacillosis ie bacterial infection in the mouth and jaw bone and elsewhere. | Antibiotic or sodium iodide intravenous weekly or potassium iodide orally daily. |
| | Consider possibility of foreign body stuck in mouth eg thorn or bramble. | Have a good look with torch and mouth gag. |

| SIGNS OF DISEASE | CAUSES | TREATMENT AND PREVENTION |
|---|---|---|
| **EYES** | | |
| Watery discharge from one or both eyes. | Entropion ie inturned eye lid. Unlikely in adult animal. | Minor surgery required. |
| White discharge from one or both eyes, sometimes with damage to the surface of the eye. | Infectious Kerato conjunctivitis due to infection by Rickettsia or Chlamydia bacteria. | Subconjuctival injection job for the vet or topical antibiotic ointment. Control is difficult. Reduce crowding. Control flies. |
| Discharge from one eye with or without eye damage. | Look for foreign body in the eye eg hay seed or similar. | Careful search required and then remove. Antibiotic ointment after removal. |
| Swollen eye lids. | Allergic reaction. | Antihistamine or corticosteriod injections. May have to move pastures. |
| Eyes dull and lifeless. | Animal may be in pain or suffering from any general ailment. | Look for other symptoms before commencing treatment. |
| Blindness with abnormalities in the lens of the eye. | Cataracts. | Surgery is possible but rarely practical. |
| Blindness with no obvious lesions in the eye. | Possible Cerebrocorical Necrosis. Due to Thiamine deficiency. | Thiamine injections are usually beneficial. |
| | Encephalitis ie brain infection or Listeriosis. | Antibiotic injections may be helpful. Need to use those that pass the blood brain barrier eg Ampicillin. |
| Yellow colour in the white of the eye. | Jaundice - usually the result of copper poisoning. This may be due to excess copper in the food but may be over medication, ie misuse of copper injection. | Oral dose of sodium sulphate may help but generally poor prognosis. |
| Membranes of the eye pale or white. | Anaemia due to worms or fluke or deficiency of iron in the diet. | Treat with anthelmintic if indicated. Iron by injection. Vit B12 also useful. |

| SIGNS OF DISEASE | CAUSES | TREATMENT AND PREVENTION |
|---|---|---|
| Membranes of the eye dark and congested. | Circulatory difficulties as part of more generalised disease, eg pneumonia or toxaemias. | Check for other symptoms. If in doubt see vet. |
| Eyes sunk into sockets. | Dehydration usually as the result of scouring. | Electrolytes and fluid therapy and treat cause of dehydration. |
| **EARS** | | |
| One or both ears swollen. | Abscess or blood blister ie haematoma. | Drain abscess and inject antibiotic. Haematoma, leave to absorb naturally but this will result in "cauliflower ear". |
| One ear drooping with possible discharge from ear canal. | No specific bacterial infection or may be Listeriosis. | Antibiotic. If Listeriosis then consider source of infection eg silage pit. Also practice good hygiene to limit spread of infection. |
| **SKIN AND COAT** | | |
| Loss of hair with itch and some skin thickening. | Mange due to Sarcoptes Scabiei or Chorioptic mange if lesions are confined to the legs or heels. Skin scrapings required for diagnosis. | Repeat washings with organophosphorous compounds or similar recommended products. |
| Itchy places around the head, ears and legs. | Sheep Scab due to Psoroptic mite infestation. | Use sheep scab dip preparations containing Diazinon or Propetamphos. |
| Loss of coat with severe itching. Parasites found. | Lice infestation. | Dip or spray or dust with recommended products eg organophosphorous compounds or Gamma benzene hexachloride. Invermectin orally. |
| Sever itching with nervous signs. | Scrapie due to infection by small virus - like particles. | No treatment. All infected animals should be slaughtered. |
| Small nodules or spots over the chest and shoulders, some irritation. | Demodectic mange infection. Skin scraping required for diagnosis. | Treatment difficult. Try malathion or rotenone compounds. |

| SIGNS OF DISEASE | CAUSES | TREATMENT AND PREVENTION |
|---|---|---|
| Loss of hair in small patches anywhere on body. Not itchy. | Ringworm usually due to Trichophyton infection. CARE, INFECTIOUS TO PEOPLE. | Oral Griseofulvin. Do not give to pregnant animals. Topical anitfungal agents. |
| Multiple skin eruptions and swellings. | Possible allergic reaction due to inhaled, ingested or contact allergen. | Antihistamine or corticosteroid injections. May need to change feed. |
| Swellings/ abscesses around the rear or hind end. | Caseous lymphadenitis due to a type of tuberculosis. Rare in UK. | No treatment effective. NOTIFIABLE DISEASE. |

## BREATHING

| | | |
|---|---|---|
| Rapid breathing. | Stress due to pain or overheating or exercise. | Remove the source of the stress and the symptoms should resolve quite quickly. |
| | Pneumonia commonly due to bacterial infection eg Pasteurellosis. | Injection of antibiotic required. Reduce stress, if indoors. Vaccine available for Pasteurella infection. |
| | Parasitic pneumonia due to lung worm infection. Many species could be involved. | Anthelmintic eg Ivermectin or Levamisole required or Fenbendazole. |
| Slow progressive onset of rapid breathing. | Rare form of C.A.E ie Caprine Arthritis and Encephalitis. | No treatment. Slaughter all affected animals. |
| Shallow breathing. | Asleep or in terminal stage of illness. | If unable to wake animal get vet ASAP. |
| Coughing. | Respiratory infection eg pneumonia. Due to infection by bacteria, virus or parasite. See above. | Antibiotic, anti inflammatory and mucolytic drugs. Anthelmintic for lung worm. Get vet to check diagnosis. |
| | Inhalation pneumonia following faulty drenching or dosing. | Antibiotic to control secondary infection. Improve drenching technique. |

## TEMPERATURE
Normal Range is
101.5-102.5 F

| | | |
|---|---|---|
| Raised. | Usually means an infection but may be the result of heat, stress or pain. Check again. May be | Check for other symptoms. If in doubt check with a vet. Antibiotic for infection. |

| SIGNS OF DISEASE | CAUSES | TREATMENT AND PREVENTION |
|---|---|---|
| Lowered. | incorrect technique or reading. If correct may be terminally ill. | Check for other symptoms eg diarrhoea. Give symptomatic treatment until diagnosis is made and warm patient up gradually. |

**DUNG**

| SIGNS OF DISEASE | CAUSES | TREATMENT AND PREVENTION |
|---|---|---|
| Constipation. | May be the result of Acetonaemia ie negative energy balance in first month after kidding. | Intravenous glucose and corticosteriods, propylene glycol or glycerine by mouth. |
| | Could also be the sequel to digestive disorders or a fever. | Laxative ie liquid paraffin or epsom salts in a bran mash. |
| Scouring. No blood in diarrhoea. | Parasitic gastro enteritis ie worms. Many species may be involved. Faecal sample required to make diagnosis. | Dose with anthelmintic and move onto clean pasture. |
| | Chronic Fasciolisis ie chronic fluke infection. | Dose with anthelmintic for fluke infection. See vet if in doubt. Drain land and get rid of snail which is the intermediate host. |
| Scouring, light in colour. | Ruminal acidosis due to animal eating too many concentrates or cereal. | Remove concentrate diet. Give carbohydrate by mouth. Multivitamins and antihistamines may help. |
| Scouring after change of diet or moving onto new pasture. | Similar to above. Nutritional upset due to change of diet or lush pasture. | Increase roughage in diet eg hay and symptoms should disappear. Change diet slowly. |
| Dung persistently soft and loose. Animal very thin. | Johnes' Disease due to infection by Mycobacterium johnei. | No treatment. Euthanase on welfare grounds. |
| Scour with occasional blood seen. | Possible Salmonella infection. INFECTIOUS TO PEOPLE. | Antibiotic and fluid therapy. Careful nursing required. Very guarded outlook. |
| Scouring with blood and mucus seen. Animal very depressed. | Enterotoxaemia due to Clostridial infection. | Antibiotic in high doses, and anti inflammatory injections plus fluid therapy. Vaccine useful to control disease. |

| SIGNS OF DISEASE | CAUSES | TREATMENT AND PREVENTION |
|---|---|---|
| Scouring, loss of colour in coat anaemia. | Consider copper or cobalt deficiency. Need blood test for diagnosis. | Give copper or cobalt by injection or orally but only after diagnosis has been reached. |

## BLOAT

| SIGNS OF DISEASE | CAUSES | TREATMENT AND PREVENTION |
|---|---|---|
| Bloat ie abdominal distention of left side of abdomen. | Gas not being belched from rumen. Could be due to obstruction ie foreign body (unlikely in goat) or failure in mechanism to allow belching. Frothy bloat (most likely type in adults) where gas and stomach contents are mixed as a froth. Frothy bloat usually caused by overeating especially on lush diet. | If bloat due to obstruction remove it or push it into the rumen. If this not possible vet will insert trocar and cannula to relieve abdominal distention. If a frothy bloat use stomach drench of silicone or vegetable oil preparations. Remove from suspect pasture or restrict access. Feed hay prior to turning out. |
| Bloat with distention on both sides of the abdomen. | Severe bloat. Animal will be close to death. | May require emergency trocarisation. Get vet. |
| Abdominal distention with mammary enlargement. | Pregnant or if has not been with male, false pregnancy. | If not pregnant, prostaglandins or corticosteroids will cause a "cloud burst" and the animal will return to normal. |

## URINE

| SIGNS OF DISEASE | CAUSES | TREATMENT AND PREVENTION |
|---|---|---|
| Diffuse swelling along belly from navel backwards with or without urine dribbling from sheath. | Urolithiasis due to calculi blocking urethra. Particularly common in male castrates. | Relaxant drugs if partial blockage. Surgery or euthanasia for severe cases. Check diet. Salt in diet may prevent new cases. |
| Discoloured urine often dark red in colour. | Clostridial infection. Rare in goats. | Antibiotic and fluid therapy. Poor prognosis. Vaccine as prevention. |
| Blood in urine. | Bacterial infection or urolithiasis or both. | Antibiotic plus see above. |
| Pain in abdomen, seen as getting up and lying down frequently, teeth grinding and kicking at belly. | Colic due to bloat, or urolithiasis or intestinal blockage. | Muscle relaxants or pain killers. Surgery if indicated will lead to poor prognosis. |

| SIGNS OF DISEASE | CAUSES | TREATMENT AND PREVENTION |
|---|---|---|
| **LAMENESS** Feet. | Bacterial infection in the foot eg Foot Rot or Foot abscess or Foot Scald. Commonly due to Fusiformis species or if abscess, Corynebacteria. | Pare foot where appropriate and dress with topical spray. Inject antibiotic when required. Keep feet dry and clean and use foot baths with formalin as prevention. |
| Blisters around the coronet. | Foot and Mouth Disease. Now rare. | Check for ulcers in mouth. If in any doubt call the vet. NOTIFIABLE DISEASE. |
| Limbs | Injury eg fracture, nerve damage, puncture wounds or strain. | All but the most minor may need vet attention. Treat as required by symptoms. |
| | Clostridial infection. eg Black Leg. Animal will be acutely ill. | Large doses of antibiotic and antisera. Vaccinate to prevent. |
| Swollen joints. | Caprine Arthritis and Encephalomyelitis ie C.A.E. | None. Euthanasia often required on welfare grounds. Keep away from all young animals. |
| | Erysipelas or other joint infections. | Antibiotic and good hygiene required. Clean pens and dips. |
| Reluctant to move on front feet, taking weight on hind. | Laminitis ie inflammation in the lamina of the foot, due to bacterial toxins in blood stream or may be just overweight or animal may have gorged on too rich a diet. | Pain killers and anti-inflammatory drugs. Bathe feet in warm water. Check diet. |
| Painful joints and stiff with tendency for bones to fracture easily. | Osteomalacia due to dietary imbalance of calcium, phosphorous and Vit D. Often the result of pregnancy and lactation. | Oral and injectable calcium and Vit D preparations. Check and maintain adequate diet. |

| SIGNS OF DISEASE | CAUSES | TREATMENT AND PREVENTION |
|---|---|---|
| **INFERTILITY**<br>**FEMALE**<br>Failure to come into season. | Pregnant. May be false pregnancy due to hormone imbalance. | Vet may be required to check for pregnancy. |
| | Low body weight or deficiency disease eg manganese or copper or Vit E/selenium. | Check diagnosis with blood samples before undertaking any treatment. |
| | Ovarian problems which in the young goat may be congenital. | If treating individual it may be worth trying treatment but if congenital cull from herd. See vet. |
| Comes into season but does not conceive. | Possible genital tract infection. | Antibiotic or cull from herd. |
| | Hormone imbalance. | May be treatable on individual basis by vet. |
| Abortion | Infection most likely cause eg Toxoplasma, Brucellosis (CARE, INFECTIOUS TO PEOPLE) Campylobacter, Listeriosis, Tick Borne Fever, Salmonella and fungal infections. | All abortions should be investigated properly. <u>Treat all as potentially hazardous to people.</u> Good hygiene is essential at all times. Isolate affected animals until a diagnosis is made. |
| | Isolated cases may be due to poor handling and clumsy management. | Check and improve on management. |
| Vaginal discharge. Clear with or without blood staining. | If pregnant, may be about to give birth or abort. Slight discharge may be apparent when in season. | Get experienced help to check. |
| Purulent smelly discharge with or without afterbirth being retained. | If not pregnant, primary infection of genital tract. If after giving birth, metritis due to infection with or without retention of afterbirth. Dead kids may still be retained in uterus. | Antibiotic by injection and in uterine pessaries or uterine irrigation. Remove retained afterbirth if possible and any retained dead kids. |

| SIGNS OF DISEASE | CAUSES | TREATMENT AND PREVENTION |
|---|---|---|
| **INFERTILITY** MALE | Specific infection of the testicle(s). | Better to cull animal than to attempt treatment. |
| | Deficiency disease eg Vit A or Zinc. | Vitamin or zinc supplements. |
| | Lameness eg sore back legs or feet making it difficult or painful for the animal to mount. | Should be self evident on careful observation. Get vet to check and treat any lameness. |
| | Sores around sheath or scrotum may inhibit mating. Check for Orf. | Localised treatment with antibiotic may help. |
| **MASTITIS** Milk very thick after kidding. | Normal colostrum. | Milk will clear after a few days. |
| Clots in milk. | Mild form of mastitis. Many bacteria might be involved but probably a streptococcus. | Intra-mammary antibiotic required. |
| Milk very watery and udder often very sore and red. | Acute mastitis due to E.coli or Pasteurella or Staphylococcus aureus. | Antibiotic, both intra-mammary and injectable. |
| Udder cold, goat very ill, blood stained fluid present at teat. | Peracute mastitis with gangrene, usually due to Staph aureus or Pasteurella infection. | May be necessary to amputate teat to allow drainage. Antibiotic, anti-inflammatory drugs and electrolytes may be required. Very grave prognosis. |
| Udder normal temperature but hard, no milk can be expressed. | Chronic mastitis. | Probably no effective treatment but try antibiotic injection. |
| | Blocked teat canal. | Get vet to check and unblock if possible. |
| Red sores over the udder area. | Orf ie virus infection. | Antibiotic will help stop spread of infection. |

| SIGNS OF DISEASE | CAUSES | TREATMENT AND PREVENTION |
|---|---|---|
| Milk Taint. Goats milk should taste similar to cows milk. | Source of taint could be food eg silage, turnips etc. | Check diet. |
| | Acetonaemia. | Fluids steroids propylene glycol. |
| | Presence of male goats poor hygiene when milking. Some medications. | Get vet to check when source is not apparent. |

**BEHAVIOUR**

| SIGNS OF DISEASE | CAUSES | TREATMENT AND PREVENTION |
|---|---|---|
| Loss of appetite. | Any infection causing a rise in temperature. | Check for other symptoms before starting treatment. |
| | Pain; check mouth for sores. Check for abdominal pain eg teeth grinding and grunting. | Treatment depends on cause of pain and definite diagnosis required see vet. |
| Slow progressive loss of appetite in pregnant animal and finally recumbency. | Pregnancy Toxaemia due to energy deficiency caused by faulty feeding procedure. Less common than in sheep. | Glycerol, propylene glycol, steroids and anabolic steroid. Abortion may be necessary. Ensure adequate diet and exercise in last half of pregnancy. |
| Slow progressive loss of appetite in lactating animal. | Acetonaemia due to negative energy balance as result of faulty feeding. | Treatment similar to that for Pregnancy Toxaemia. |
| Fairly sudden loss of appetite and then recumbency in later pregnancy and after kidding. | Hypocalcaemia due to lack of calcium in circulation. | Give calcium intravenously or under the skin. |
| Recumbency with fits and foaming at the mouth. | Hypomagnesaemia due to low levels of magnesium in the blood stream. More common on lush pasture after kidding. | Magnesium injection given under the skin. Feed magnesium rich food. Restrict time on lush pasture. Magnesium boluses. |
| Walking in circles and head pressing. | Middle Ear infection or Listeriosis. | Antibiotic. Avoid silage feeding. Good hygiene essential at kidding time as Listerella can cause abortions. |
| | Gid (Sturdy) ie Tapeworm cyst in brain. | Surgery to remove cyst. Routine tape worm dosing of all dogs. |

| SIGNS OF DISEASE | CAUSES | TREATMENT AND PREVENTION |
| --- | --- | --- |
| Head pressing with peculiar high stepping gait, then recumbency. | Louping Ill due to virus infection. | Antisera may be useful if used early. Vaccine available. Control the tick which is the intermediate host. |
| Progressive lameness with swollen joints and eventual paralysis. | Caprine Arthritis and Encephalitis (CAE) due to virus infection. | No treatment. Isolate all infected animals. Blood test available. |
| Intense itch with loss of condition despite good appetite, recumbency head raised with lip nibbling. | Scrapie due to infection by small virus like particles. | Slaughter all affected animals. |
| General stiffness, anxious and often immobile. | Tetanus due to infection by Clostridium tentani in wound. | Antisera antibiotic sedation. Vaccine available. |
| **SUDDEN DEATH** | Anthrax ie infection with Bacillus anthracis. | Rare. Source of infection usually contaminated feed. NOTIFIABLE DISEASE AND INFECTIOUS TO PEOPLE. |
| | Any of the Clostridial diseases eg Enterotoxaemia. | Vaccines are available and effective. |
| | Plant poisoning eg Yew or Laurel. | Goats are very inquisitive. Never leave hedge or tree clippings where animal can reach them. |
| | Lightning Strike or electrocution. | Post mortem should be able to show scorch marks on the skin. CARE IF ELECTROCUTION IS SUSPECTED. GET QUALIFIED PERSON TO CHECK ALL ELECTRIC FITTINGS. |

# A GUIDE TO ANIMAL AILMENTS AND TREATMENT — KIDS

| SIGNS OF DISEASE | CAUSES | TREATMENT AND PREVENTION |
|---|---|---|
| **HEAD AND FACE** Nasal Discharge. | Pneumonia due to virus or bacterial infection. | Antibiotic. Check environment for overcrowding and if indoors, ventilation. If outdoors, check shelter provision in bad weather. |
| | If newly born and just beginning to suckle, check for cleft palate. | If defect is severe euthanase. Check with vet. |
| Ulcers on lips, tongue and dental pad. | Foot and Mouth Disease (unlikely to be seen only in kids) now rare. | Check for other symptoms eg blisters around feet. If suspicious inform vet or Ministry. NOTIFIABLE DISEASE. |
| Scabs on lips also on nostrils and eye lids. | Orf ie infection by Paravaccinia virus. | Topical ointments and sprays can stop secondary bacterial infection. Isolate affected animals. Vaccine available. |
| Scabs on face ie around eye ears and base of horns. | Facial eczema due to bacterial infection ie Staphylococcus aureus. More uncommon in goats than sheep. | Antibiotic. Check trough space is adequate. |
| | Above condition may be complicated by Fly Worry. | Insecticides can be used or head protected by headcap. |
| Loss of hair on face especially around the eyes. | Ringworm, usually due to Trichophyton verrucosum. Rare condition but more common than in sheep. CARE, INFECTIOUS TO PEOPLE. | Topical and oral antifungal agents. |

| SIGNS OF DISEASE | CAUSES | TREATMENT AND PREVENTION |
|---|---|---|
| Salivation and drooling from the mouth. | Viral infection eg Orf or Foot and Mouth. See above. | See above. |
| | Actinobacillosis ie bacterial infection in the mouth and jaw bone and elsewhere. Uncommon in young animal. | Antibiotic or sodium iodide intravenous once weekly or potassium iodide orally daily. |
| | Colibacillosis ie Watery Mouth. Due to infection by Ecoli. | Antibiotic and Metoclopramide and electrolytes. Ensure good colostrum intake. Good hygiene essential. |
| | Consider possibility of foreign body stuck in mouth eg bramble or thorn. | Have a good look, with torch and mouth gag if necessary. |
| **EYES** Watery discharge from one or both eyes. | Entropion ie inturned eye lid(s). | Easily rectified with minor surgery by vet. If a major problem in herd look at breeding programme. |
| White discharge from one or both eyes sometimes with damage to the surface of the eye. | Infectious Kerato-Conjunctivitis due to infection by Rickettsia or Chlamydia organism. | Subconjuctival injection (job for the vet) or topical antibiotic ointment. Control is difficult. Reduce crowding. Control flies. |
| Discharge from one eye with or without eye damage. | Look for foreign body in the eye eg hay seed or similar. | Careful search and remove and then administer antibiotic eye ointment. |
| Swollen eye lids. | Allergic reaction. | Antihistamine or corticosteroids. May have to move pastures. |
| Eyes dull and lifeless. | Animal may be in pain or suffering from any general ailment. | Look for other symptoms before commencing treatment. |
| Blindness with abnormalities in the lens. | Congenital cataracts. | Nothing practical can be done. |

| SIGNS OF DISEASE | CAUSES | TREATMENT AND PREVENTION |
|---|---|---|
| Blindness with no obvious lesions in the eye. | Possible Cerebrocortical Necrosis. Due to Thiamine deficiency. | Thiamine injections are often helpful. |
| | Encephalitis ie brain infection or Listeriosis. | Antibiotic injections may be helpful. Need to use those that pass the blood brain barrier eg ampicillin. |
| Yellow colour in the white of the eye. | Jaundice usually the result of copper poisoning. This is usually due to excessive amounts in the feed. | Oral dose of sodium sulphate may help but generally poor prognosis. |
| Membranes of the eye pale or white. | Anaemia due to worms or deficiency of iron in the diet. | Treat with anthelmintic. Iron by injection B12 also helpful. |
| Membranes of the eye dark and congested. | Circulatory difficulties as part of more generalised disease eg pneumonia. | Check for other symptoms and treat for general disease. See vet. |
| Eyes sunk into eye sockets. | Dehydration usually as the result of scouring. | Electrolytes as fluid replacer and treat the cause of the scour. |
| **EARS** One or both ears swollen. | Abscess or blood blister (haematoma). | Drain abscess and give antibiotic. Blood blister lead to absorb naturally. This will distort the ear. |
| One ear drooping with possible discharge from ear canal. | Bacterial infection. Possible Listeriosis. | Antibiotic. If Listeriosis consider source of infection eg silage. Also practice good hygiene at kidding time to limit spread of infection. |
| **SKIN AND COAT** Loss of hair with itch and some skin thickening. | Mange due to Sarcoptes Scabiei. Or Chorioptic mange if lesions confined to legs or heels. | Repeat washing with organo-phosphorous compounds or similar recommended products. |
| Itchy places around head ears and legs. | Sheep Scab due to Psoroptic mite infestation. | Use sheep scab dip containing diazinon or propetamphos. |
| Loss of coat with severe itching. Parasites found. | Lice infestation very common in goats. | Dip or spray infected animals with recommended products eg organo-phosphorous compounds or Gamma benzene hexachloride. |

| SIGNS OF DISEASE | CAUSES | TREATMENT AND PREVENTION |
|---|---|---|
| Small nodules or spots over the shoulder and chest some irritation. | Demodectic mange infection. | Treatment difficult. Try malathion or rotenone compounds. |
| Loss of hair in small patches any where on body. Not itchy. | Ringworm, usually due to Trichophyton infection. CARE, INFECTIOUS TO PEOPLE. | Oral Griseofulvin (care do not feed to pregnant animals) or topical antifungal agents. |
| Multiple skin eruptions and swellings. | Possible allergic reaction due to inhaled, ingested or contact allergen. | Antihistamines corticosteroids. Change feed. |

**BREATHING**

| | | |
|---|---|---|
| Rapid breathing. | Pneumonia usually due to bacterial infection eg Pasteurellosis. | Antibiotic. Reduce stress, check ventilation Vaccine available. |
| | Stress due to pain overheating, or exercise. | Remove the source of the stress and the symptoms should resolve quickly. |
| Shallow breathing. | Asleep or in terminal stages of illness. | If unable to wake check for other symptoms and get vet. |
| Coughing. | Respiratory disease eg pneumonia. | Antibiotic, anti-inflammatory drugs and mucolytics. |
| | Inhalation pneumonia following faulty drenching and dosing. | Antibiotic to control secondary infection. Improve dosing technique. |

**TEMPERATURE**
Normal range is 101.5-102.5 F.

| | | |
|---|---|---|
| Raised. | Usually means an infection has set in but could be due to pain, stress or weather conditions. | Check for other symptoms. If in doubt check with vet. Antibiotic for infection. |
| Lowered. | Check again. May be incorrect reading or technique. Hypothermia can be a killer in young kids. Animal may be terminally ill. | Raise body temperature with heat lamps or equivalent. Check for other symptoms eg diarrhoea. |

| SIGNS OF DISEASE | CAUSES | TREATMENT AND PREVENTION |
|---|---|---|
| Shivering. | May be early stages of hypothermia. | See above. Check for draughts if indoors. If outdoors, is there adequate shelter. Has the youngster fed recently? |

## DUNG

| SIGNS OF DISEASE | CAUSES | TREATMENT AND PREVENTION |
|---|---|---|
| Constipation. | Uncommon but can be one of symptoms of wet mouth (diarrhoea is more common). | Check for other symptoms. Liquid paraffin useful 1-2 teaspoons full. |
| Scouring. Young kids, no blood in diarrhoea. | Bacterial (eg E.coli) or viral infection (eg Rotavirus). | Antibiotic and electrolytes. Keep the patient warm. Colostrum essential for prevention as is good hygiene. |
| Scouring with blood in diarrhoea, animal very ill. | Enterotoxaemia due to Clostridial infection. | Antibiotic and anti-inflammatory injections plus electrolytes. Keep the patient warm. Vaccine useful to control disease. |
| Kid at least 3-4 weeks old with diarrhoea, some blood may be present. | Coccidiosis usually infection with Eimeria species. | Oral anitbacterials eg Amprolium of sulphadimidine. Avoid overcrowding and wet areas. Prophylactic medication in the feed may be used. |
| Older kids with diarrhoea, no blood. | Parasitic Gastro-enteritis ie worms. These include Haemonchus, Ostertagia, Trichostrongylus Nematodirus and Oesophagostomum species. | Anthelmintic to all affected animals. Put onto worm free pasture after worming the kids. |
| Diarrhoea with no signs of infection. | Nutritional scour due to lush pasture or sudden increase in feed. | Remove from diet and put onto hay and water diet until recovered. |

## BLOAT

| SIGNS OF DISEASE | CAUSES | TREATMENT AND PREVENTION |
|---|---|---|
| Bloat ie abdominal distention of left side of abdomen. | Gas not being belched from rumen or abomasum (true stomach). Could be due to obstruction in gullet or failure of the belching mechanism, or frothy bloat where gas and fluid are mixed as a froth. | Dose with silicone or oil preparations. Pass stomach tube if necessary. Get vet to check diet. If bloat due to lush diet of lucerne or clover, remove from pasture and feed hay and water when distention is relieved. |

| SIGNS OF DISEASE | CAUSES | TREATMENT AND PREVENTION |
|---|---|---|
| Bloat with distention on both sides of abdomen. | Uncommon in young kids except those bottled fed. Severe bloat. Animal will be close to death. | Emergency. May required trocarisation. Get vet. |
| Swelling under belly at navel. | Naval infection. | Antibiotic. Dip navel at birth with iodine or spray with antibiotic. |
| | Umbilical hernia. | If small, no action required. If large, surgery may be required. |

## URINE

| SIGNS OF DISEASE | CAUSES | TREATMENT AND PREVENTION |
|---|---|---|
| Diffuse swelling under navel in older kids. | Urolithiasis due to calculi blocking urethra. | Relaxant drugs if partial blockage. Surgery or euthanasia for severe cases. Check diet. Salt in diet may prevent new cases. |
| Discoloured urine often dark red in colour. | Clostridial infection. Rare in kids. | Antibiotic and fluid therapy. Poor prognosis vaccine are to prevent. |
| Pain in abdomen seen as lying down and getting up frequently, teeth grinding and kicking. | Colic due to bloat, urolithiasis or intestinal blockage. | Muscle relaxants, pain killers. Surgery if indicated will give a poor prognosis. |

## LAMENESS

| SIGNS OF DISEASE | CAUSES | TREATMENT AND PREVENTION |
|---|---|---|
| Feet. | Bacterial infection in the foot eg foot rot, foot abscess or foot scald. Commonly due to Fusiformis species or if abscess, Corynebacteria. Virus infection eg Foot and Mouth Disease. | Pare foot where appropriate and dress with topical spray. Inject antibiotic. Keep feet dry and clean and use foot baths with 5% formalin as prevention. Check for ulcers in mouth. If in doubt call the vet. NOTIFIABLE DISEASE. |
| Limbs | Injury eg fracture, nerve damage, puncture wounds or strain. | All but the most minor may need vet attention. Treat as required by symptoms. |
| | Clostridial infection eg Black Leg. Rare in young goats. | Large doses of antibiotic and antisera. Vaccinate to prevent. |
| Swollen joints. | Joint Ill ie bacterial infection in the joint(s). eg Erysipelas or C. pyogenes. | Antibiotic and good hygiene required. Clean pens and foot dips. Dip navels at birth in iodine or spray with antibiotic. |

| SIGNS OF DISEASE | CAUSES | TREATMENT AND PREVENTION |
|---|---|---|
| Deformed limbs. | Rickets due to imbalance of calcium, phosphorous and Vit D. | Oral and injectable calcium and Vit D preparations. Check and maintain adequate diet. |
| Softening of jaw bones and frequent fractures. | Excess phosphorous in the diet. | Give extra calcium and ensure a balanced diet. |
| Stiff limbs and sometimes difficulty in standing. | Vitamin E selenium deficiency. | Vit E and selenium injections. Nutritional supplements. |

**BEHAVIOUR**

| | | |
|---|---|---|
| Loss of appetite. | Any infection causing a rise in temperature. | Check for other symptoms before starting any treatment. |
| | Pain; check mouth for sores; check for abdominal pain. Pain causing lameness is unlikely to cause loss of appetite. | Treatment depends on cause of pain. Pain killers, anti-inflammatory drugs and antibiotic may all be helpful. |
| Kids born weak with tremors and hair abnormalities. | Border Disease due to viral infection. | No treatment. Isolate all infected animals and their mothers who will be carrying the infection. |
| Progressive hind leg paralysis with lameness and swollen joints in older kids. | Caprine Arthritis Encephalomyelitis due to viral infection. | No treatment. Isolate all infected animals. |
| Born dead or weak with incoordinated leg movements and swaying. | Swayback. Due to copper deficiency in the mother. | Very little can be done for clinical cases. Prevent by giving mother copper injections or boluses or oral copper supplements. |
| Blindness and walking in circles in older kids. | Cerebrocorticl necrosis due to thiamine deficiency. | High levels of thiamine by injection. |
| Walking in circles and head pressing. | Middle ear infection or Listeriosis. | Antibiotic. Avoid silage. Good hygiene essential at kidding time. |

| SIGNS OF DISEASE | CAUSES | TREATMENT AND PREVENTION |
|---|---|---|
| Head pressing with peculiar gait, then recumbency. | Louping Ill due to virus infection. | Antisera may be useful if used early. Vaccine available. Control ticks which are the intermediate host. |
| Kids dull and weak usually within a few hours or days of birth. | Hypothermia as the result of bad weather or inadequate feeding. | Rewarm gently. Feed by stomach tube if cannot suckle. Provide adequate shelter and make sure the youngster has had an adequate colostrum intake. |
| **SUDDEN DEATH** | Anthrax ie infection with Bacillus anthracis. | Rare, as source of infection is usually contaminated feed. CARE, NOTIFIABLE DISEASE AND INFECTIOUS TO PEOPLE. |
| | Any of the Clostridial Diseases eg Enterotoxaemia. | Vaccines are available and effective. |
| | Plant poisoning eg Yew or Laurel. | Kids are very inquisitive. Never leave hedge or tree clippings where animals can reach them. |
| | Lightning strike or electrocution. | Post mortem should be able to show scorch marks on the skin. CARE, IF ELECTROCUTION IS SUSPECTED GET QUALIFIED PERSON TO CHECK ALL ELECTRIC FITTINGS. |

# HORSES

Many of the afflictions that beset horses and ponies are the result of domestication. Evolution created the Equine to graze small amounts of grass and keep moving. They are not solitary creatures and like to be part of a herd. It is not surprising when they are cooped up for long hours, sometimes without sight of a fellow creature, that they are subject to all manner of behavioural vices such as wind sucking, crib biting and weaving.

With nothing else to do they will eat their bedding, even if it is a poor quality straw, which can lead to constipation and colic. Ponies and some horses too, if allowed to graze on too succulent grass, without any exercise, develop laminitis. This can result in severe distress and pain and may mean an end to the useful life of the animal or death if suffering can not be alleviated by treatment.

Stables and loose boxes are notorious for being very poorly ventilated. It is a common belief that a half open stable door will supply sufficient fresh air and this is just not true. There has been a huge increase in the incidence Chronic Obstructive Pulmonary Disease. This is an allergic condition, similar to asthma in people which is caused by sensitivity to hay spores. Poor ventilation in the stable often makes the condition much worse and may indeed be the reason the animal was sensitised in the first place. With chronic sufferers the best and cheapest treatment is fresh air. Afflicted animals are best kept outside with a field shelter and New Zealand rug for protection in the winter weather. Hay, if fed at all, has to be soaked to denature the fungal spores otherwise vacuum packed ensilaged grass has to be used.

It is positively criminal not to vaccinate any horse or pony against Tetanus. Clostridial spores are thick on the ground wherever Equines graze and Tetanus, once clinical symptoms appear, still has a very poor survival rate. It is not good enough to wait until an animal suffers a wound and then vaccinate or give Tetanus anti serum. You should, o course, do this if the animal is injured and previously unprotected but many cases of Tetanus occur where no visible wound has been seen.

# A GUIDE TO ANIMAL AILMENTS AND
# TREATMENT — HORSES

| SIGNS OF DISEASE | CAUSES | TREATMENT AND PREVENTION |
|---|---|---|
| **HEAD AND FACE**<br>Nasal discharge thin, grey from one or both nostrils with cough. | Possible virus infection eg Equine Flu or Equine Herpes. | Antibiotic to protect against secondary pneumonia. Mucolytic and bronchodilators. Good hygiene and nursing essential. Vaccine available against Equine Flu. |
| | Chronic Obstructive Pulmonary Disease (COPD) due to allergic reaction to fungal spores. | Bronchodilators and mucolytic drugs eg Ventipulmin (Clenbuterol), Sputolosin. (Boehringer). Soak hay and provide dust and allergen-free environment. |
| Yellow purulent discharge from one or both nostrils. | Strangles due to Streptococcus equi or similar infection due to Streptococcus zooepidemicus. Infection may extend to guttural pouch. | Penicillin still drug of choice. Strict hygiene and isolation required. Very infectious. |
| Non-specific discharge. | Usually infection in upper respiratory tract or sinus due to a variety of bacteria. Consider also possibility of pneumonia if animal is breathing heavily. | Need nasal swab to check type of bacteria. Antibiotic and mucolytics are helpful. Good nursing and hygiene is a must. |
| Food material coming down nostril, animal with neck outstretched. | Gullet choked with food material usually caused by feeding dry food eg sugar beet. | Most cases respond to sedatives and muscle relaxants. Severe cases may require stomach tube and siphoning. |

| SIGNS OF DISEASE | CAUSES | TREATMENT AND PREVENTION |
|---|---|---|
| Salivation and dribbling from mouth sometimes with green discharge from nostrils. | Grass Sickness, cause unknown. Due to degeneration of nerves to gut. | No specific treatment available. More common in horses 2 years old and over at grass and in summer months. Supportive treatment only. |
| Salivation and dribbling from mouth. | Check for damage due to trauma eg damage from the bit. | Salt water bathing for mouth sores. Get experienced person to check bridle and bit. |
| | Check teeth for sharp points and edges. | Vet to check teeth and rasp if necessary. |
| | Mouth ulcers due to virus or bacterial infection. | Salt water mouth washes. Antibiotic may be required. |
| Unable to swallow, dribbling with a general stiffness and apprehension. | Early signs of Tetanus due to infection by Clostridium tetani. | High doses of antibiotic, antiserum and sedatives. Very poor prognoses vaccination is essential. |
| Nose bleed, from one nostril. | Usually trauma or common sequel to passing stomach tube. | Usually stops spontaneously. Looks worse than it often appears. |
| Profuse haemorrhage from nostrils. | Bleeding from internal carotid artery due to fungal infection in guttural pouch. | Frequently fatal. Surgical ligation of internal carotid artery. |
| Minor bleeding from nostrils after or during exercise. | Source of haemorrhage is usually the lungs. Horse will often have mild COPD symptoms. | Horse will need endoscope investigation. Complete rest is a must. Treat COPD. |
| Loss of hair with scabs. Round lesions. | Ringworm due to Trichophyton or Microsporum species CARE, INFECTIOUS TO PEOPLE. | Griseofulvin orally is best treatment. Must not be given to pregnant mares. Topical treatments can be used. |
| Sores and redness on white parts of face and muzzle. | Sunburn and or photosensitisation. Eating some, plants eg St John's Wort or clover can predispose to condition. | Remove from sunlight. Use sun blocks eg calamine on sore areas. Moving field away from predisposing plants. |
| Hard swelling under jaw. | Tooth abscess. | Extraction and antibiotic. |

| SIGNS OF DISEASE | CAUSES | TREATMENT AND PREVENTION |
|---|---|---|
| Soft swelling between jaw bones. | Lymph gland swelling due to infection. | Check source of infection. Antibiotic may be required. |
| Swelling at angle of jaw. Horse unwell with temperature. | Probable bacterial infection eg Strangles or similar. | Often better to allow abscess to burst before giving antibiotic. |
| Swelling at angle of jaw which comes and goes. Animal is well. | Salivary gland reacting to different feeds, usually grass. | Nothing required to be done. Horse usually comes in from grass with glands enlarged and goes down overnight. |

**EYES**

| | | |
|---|---|---|
| Discharge from one or both eyes. | Conjunctivitis due to bacterial infection or secondary to virus or bacterial infection. eg Flu or Strangles. | Topical antibiotic drops or ointment. If part of other systemic infection, patient will need treatment for the infection as well as local treatment on the eyes. |
| Discharge from one eye. | Conjunctivitis which may be due to infection or trauma or a foreign body (eg hay seed) in the eye. | Topical antibiotic treatment. Make sure there is no foreign body in the eye. |
| Swollen eye lids with discharge. | Could be just infection but consider possibility of allergic reaction. | Antibiotic topically or if part of allergic reaction may need to use corticosteroid or anti-histamine injections. |
| Recurrent eye discharge with photophobia. | Periodic ophthalmia, cause obscure. | Topical antibiotic and steroid drops. Stable away from bright light. |
| Eyes dull and lifeless. | Animal may be in pain or have a general systemic illness. | Check for other symptoms before treatment. If in doubt get the vet. |
| Blindness with opacities in the centre of the eye. | Cataracts. Common in the older horse. | Surgery is possible but rarely practical. |
| Surface of eye opaque. | Keratitis due to infection or trauma. | Antibiotic and steroid topical preparations. |
| Blindness with no apparent eye defects. | Diffuse or focal brain lesion eg abscess or tumour. | Nothing practical can be done. |

| SIGNS OF DISEASE | CAUSES | TREATMENT AND PREVENTION |
|---|---|---|
| Blindness with other nervous symptoms, eg wandering aggression, head pressing. | Acute Ragwort poisoning. | Nothing practical can be done. Euthanase. Pull up and destroy the plant or use chemical sprays. |
| Yellow colour in white of eye. | Jaundice due to chronic liver disease or chronic Ragwort poisoning. | Supportive therapy required eg B Vitamins and carbohydrates. |
|  | Bile duct obstruction due to blockage by Roundworms or Liver Fluke. | Anthelmintic can be useful. Oxyclozanide reported effective against Fluke. |
|  | Fatty liver due to overweight. Common in ponies. | Attention to diet is important. Methionine can help. |
| Membranes of eye pale and white. | Anaemia due to worms or lice or diet. | Make a definite diagnosis first then deworm and or kill lice. Improve diet and give iron and vitamin supplement. |
| Membranes of eye dark and congested. | Circulatory problems as part of a general systemic problem eg Colic or toxaemia. | Almost always a poor prognosis. Get vet to check as a matter of urgency. |
| Eyes sunk into eye sockets. | Dehydration as the result usually of scouring or debilitating illness. | Electrolytes as fluid therapy. Diagnose the cause of scour or illness and treat accordingly. |
| **EARS** Discharge from one or both ears with head shaking. | Bacterial or mite infection. | Dog ear drops. Not licensed for use in horses but often used. |
| White plaques or spots on inside of ear. | Calcium plaques. Cause not known. | No treatment required. Not harmful. |
| **SKIN AND HAIR** Loss of coat with wet crusty lesions on back, legs or quarters. | Rain scald or Mud Fever due to Dermatophilus infection. | Provide shelter to dry coat. Antibiotic may be necessary both by injection, orally or topically. Povidone iodine or chlorhexidine skin scrubs are useful. |

| SIGNS OF DISEASE | CAUSES | TREATMENT AND PREVENTION |
|---|---|---|
| Raised patches of hair with round dry crusty lesions, sometimes wet in the centre. | Ringworm due to Trichophyton or Microsporum spp. CARE, INFECTIOUS TO PEOPLE. | Topical antifungal agents or oral griseofulvin. Do not feed to pregnant mares. Keep rugs and grooming equipment and tack disinfected to avoid spread of infection. |
| Loss of hair in mane and elsewhere parasites seen. | Ectoparasites eg lice or harvest mites. | Parasitic dusting powder or skin washes. |
| Loss of hair at mane and base of tail. | Sweet Itch due to allergic reaction to biting midge. | Midge repellents. Long-acting steroids in difficult cases. Stable when midge is active ie dawn and dusk. |
| Loss of hair at base of tail. | Oxyuris equi infection causes itch at base of tail. | Any modern dewormer is effective. |
| Raised sore areas on non-pigmented part of skin eg face and legs. | Photosensitisation due to sunlight. Animal is made more sensitive by eating St John's Wort or clover. | Remove from direct sunlight. Sun block creams or calamine lotion may be useful. May be necessary to protect sensitive areas against flies. |
| Small growths on skin surface particularly on muzzle. | Warts due to virus infection. | No action required. Will self-cure. |
| Skin tumours on any part of body. | Sarcoids probably due to virus infection. | Remove surgically. BCG vaccine may be required around eyes. Cryosurgery can be useful. |
| Tumours or growths in the perennial region. | Melanomas. Common in grey horses and ponies. | Surgery only remedy. May spread internally to other organs. |
| Sudden appearance large raised areas over most of the body. | Allergic reaction due to insect bites or rolling in nettle patch. | Antihistamines or corticosteroid . Sedation may be required. |
| Small nodules over any part of the body. | Reaction to biting flies ie Myiasis. | Fly repellents. |

| SIGNS OF DISEASE | CAUSES | TREATMENT AND PREVENTION |
|---|---|---|
| Small or larger nodules in saddle area. | Saddle sores due ill fitting tack. | Get saddle checked by expert. Ointments and creams may help. |
| Small eggs deposited on hairs of neck and legs in late summer and autumn. | Bot eggs deposited by Gastrophilus species. | These can be difficult to remove. Deworm animal November to January with wormer with boticidal action. eg Ivermectin (Eqvalan). |
| Wet itchy places on legs with dandruff. | Chorioptic mange due to mite infection. Most common in heavy breeds with hairy legs. | Topical antimange shampoos eg dog washes commonly used, Ivermectin (Eqvalan) can be effective. Difficult to eradicate completely. |
| Acute wet skin infection around external genitalia of mares and stallions. | Coital eczema due to Equine Herpes type 3 infection. Transmitted at coitus. | Sexual rest for 2-3 weeks. Antibiotic may be required for secondary infection. |

**BREATHING**

| | | |
|---|---|---|
| Rapid breathing. | Pneumonia possibly due to virus infection eg Flu or Herpes and then a secondary bacterial infection. | Antibiotic and anti-inflammatory drugs, bronchodilating and mucolytic drugs also useful. Careful nursing and good ventilation is essential. |
| | Chronic Obstructive Pulmonary Disease (COPD) due to allergic response to inhaled fungal spores. | Bronchodilating and mucolytic drugs most useful. Corticosteroids. Provide dust free atmosphere and soak hay or feed vacuum packed grass. |
| | Stress due to pain, heat or over exercise. | Remove source of stress and condition should resolve quickly. |
| Dry cough. | Respiratory infection most commonly due to virus infection. eg Flu or Herpes infection. | Treat symptoms with bronchodilating and mucolytic drugs. eg Ventipulmin (Clenbuterol) and Sputolosin (Boehringer). Antibiotic to guard against secondary bacterial infection. Vaccine available against Flu. Herpes vaccine not effective against respiratory infection. |

| SIGNS OF DISEASE | CAUSES | TREATMENT AND PREVENTION |
|---|---|---|
| Soft cough. | Bacterial infection eg Strangles or other Streptococcal infection. Can often lead onto bronchopneumonia. | Penicillin is still drug of choice for any Streptococcal infection. Strict isolation of infected animal and disinfect, tack stables and equipment. Good ventilation and nursing is all important. |
| Chronic cough. | Lungworm infection. Still common when grazed with donkeys. | Febendazole and Ivermectin are both effective drugs to treat infection. |

**TEMPERATURE**
Normal is 100.5 F

| | | |
|---|---|---|
| Raised. | Usually means animal has an infection either viral or bacterial but can be the result of pain eg colic or 'tying up' syndrome. | Diagnosis needs to be made. If in doubt see vet. |
| | Can also be raised after exercise or stress eg travelling. | If due to exercise or heat stress rub down vigorously and symptoms should disappear. |
| Lowered. | Check reading again, may be faulty technique. Animal may be in poor body condition in adverse weather conditions. Scouring may also be a factor. | If correct, rub animal down vigorously and protect with rug. If outdoors in wet weather make sure rug is waterproof eg New Zealand type. Check for scour and make sure animal is eating. |
| Shivering. | May just be due to inclement weather effect on a thin skinned horse eg Arab or Thoroughbred. Should not happen in indoor animal except if animal is ill. | Mild shivering can be easily rectified if due to adverse weather or lack of feed. Thin-skinned animals will need waterproof rugs if outdoors in winter months. |
| Sweating. | Unlikely due to infection and running a temperature. More likely due to exercise, stress or colic. | Check for other symptoms. Any sign of pain due to colic get vet. If due to exercise rub down vigorously with hay wisp and protect from a chill by putting on a light rug. |

| SIGNS OF DISEASE | CAUSES | TREATMENT AND PREVENTION |
|---|---|---|
| **DUNG**<br>Constipation. | Inability to pass dung in normal quantities. Mostly due to unsuitable diet eg eating straw bedding. Can often lead to colic symptoms. | Mild cases often respond to warm bran mashes. Cases that develop into colic will need vet attention. Stomach tube saline solutions or liquid paraffin. |
| **SCOURING**<br>Dung green and like cow pats. | Dietary. Probably just turned out onto fresh grass. | Nothing needs to be done if animal is well. |
| Dung normal colour but loose. | Parasitism often due to sudden emergence of large numbers of Strongyle larvae. | Need to use larvicidal doses of anthelmintic. eg Double dose of Fenbedalous daily for 5 days or Ivermelin. |
| Sudden onset, water, profuse, foul smelling diarrhoea. | Colitis 'X' cause often unknown but sometimes drug induced. | Supportive treatment eg electrolytes, steroids and anti-diarrhoea eg kaolin.<br>Very poor prognosis. |
|  | Toxaemia from Clostridial infection. | Treatment as for Colitis 'X'. Very poor prognosis. |
| Soft faeces sometimes with blood. | Salmonella infection. CARE, CAN BE INFECTIOUS TO PEOPLE. | Antibiotic, electrolytes and good nursing.<br>Isolate cases and be strict with hygiene. Vet will attempt with lab to find source of outbreak. |
| Dung normal in appearance but with small red worms seen. Animal often looks unthrifty. | Strongylosis ie due to infection with Strongyle species of worm. | Anthelmintic. Horses and ponies should be dewormed every 4-6 weeks.<br>Rotate and rest pastures, pick up droppings. Harrow fields in dry weather. Mixed grazing with sheep and cattle. |
| Dung normal with white segments seen in droppings. | Tapeworm infection ie Anaplocephala perfoliata. | Double normal dose of Pyrantel. |

| SIGNS OF DISEASE | CAUSES | TREATMENT AND PREVENTION |
|---|---|---|
| **URINARY SYSTEM** | | |
| Mare voiding urine and 'winking' external genitalia in presence of other horses. | In season. | Season will last up to 6 days and will be repeated during Spring and early Summer ever 21 days unless she becomes pregnant. |
| Repeated straining to pass urine. | Cystitis ie bacterial infection of the bladder. | Antibiotic will clear infection. Salt in diet may help prevent recurrence. |
| | Urinary calculi ie stone in bladder or urethra. | Smooth muscle relaxant drugs. Surgery may be required. |
| Excessive thirst and passing of large quantities of dilute urine. | Kidney disease. Uncommon in horses but when it occurs will be due to bacterial infection. | Antibiotic and anabolic steroids. Prognosis may be poor. |
| Urine dark brown or blood coloured. Patient stiff and reluctant to move. | Azoturia or Exertion Myopathy due to exertion induced damage to muscles. | Sedatives, pain killers and anti-inflammatory drugs. Electrolytes. Check diet to ensure balance of minerals is correct. |
| **ABDOMINAL PAIN** | | |
| Seen as lack of appetite, groaning, sweating, kicking at belly, rolling, etc. | Colic. Variety of causes. Can be due to flatulence due to gas in belly from unsuitable feed. Constipation, see above. | Most mild cases of colic will respond to pain killing and muscle relaxant drugs. If due to constipation see above. |
| | Spasmodic colic due to migrating strongyle larvae. | Colic due to worms need treatment with larvicidal doses of anthelmintic. |
| | Abdominal catastrophe eg twisted bowel. | Abdominal catastrophe need emergency surgery or euthanasia on welfare grounds. |
| Abdominal pain with food coming down nostril. Chronic condition. | Grass sickness due to possible neuro-toxin damage to nerve supply to stomach. | Supportive treatment only. Until recently no hope of cure. Euthanasia on welfare grounds. |

| SIGNS OF DISEASE | CAUSES | TREATMENT AND PREVENTION |
|---|---|---|
| Abdominal pain with scouring. | Dietary, scour due to ingestion of unsuitable feed stuffs. | Spasmolytic (or antispasmodic) drugs and electrolytes. Remove from source of food. |
| | Salmonella infection. CARE, INFECTIOUS TO PEOPLE. | Antibiotic, electrolytes and strict hygienic precautions. |
| | Strongylosis, ie worms. | Anthelmintic preparations. See above. |
| **INFERTILITY** FEMALE. Failure to come into season. | Pregnant. | Get vet to check by urine or blood sample or by rectal ultra sound examination. |
| | Wrong time of year. | Mares only normally come into season in Spring and Summer. |
| | Ovarian disorder eg persistent corpus luteum. | Prostaglandin treatment will usually bring mare into season. |
| | Young animal that has never come into season may have congenital disorder. | Blood sample will help in diagnosis. |
| Mare in season all the time. | Failure to ovulate or nymphomania. | Chronic Gomadotrophin given intravenously will normally cause ovulation. |
| Normal season but failure to conceive. | Infection in genital tract eg Klebsiella and Pseudomonas. Windsucking into vagina may predispose to infection. | Uterine irrigation and antibiotic infusions. Surgery may be required to correct windsucking ie Caslicks operation. |
| Vaginal discharge. | Bacterial infection ie Endometritis. Any number of bacteria may be involved. Also consider Contagious Equine Metritis if Thoroughbred horse. | Intravaginal irrigations and antibiotic infusions. Strict hygiene precautions to stop venereal spread. |

| SIGNS OF DISEASE | CAUSES | TREATMENT AND PREVENTION |
|---|---|---|
| **ABORTION** | Foetal abnormalities or twins. | Detect twins and abort at early pregnancy. |
| | Viral infection eg Equine Herpes 1 or Equine Viral Arteritis. | No treatment. Vaccine available for both conditions. Strict hygiene necessary. |
| | Bacterial or fungal infection. | Uterus may require antibiotic therapy to avoid chronic infertility. |
| **INFERTILITY** MALE Lack of libido. | Immaturity. Not very likely as most colts are fairly precocious. | Matings must be well supervised to make sure young animal is not injured or inhibited by older animal. |
| | Orthopaedic problems eg sore back, legs or pelvis can inhibit copulation. | Get vet to check and treat any lameness. |
| | Also consider age, poor nutrition and intercurrent disease. | Get vet to check. |
| Libido good but failure to get mare in foal. | Fertility lowered or nil due to infection in genital tract eg bacterial infection in testicles (orchitis). | Prognosis for future fertility very guarded. Try antibiotic. Check sperm count. |
| Covering normal but mare develops vaginal discharge after a few days. | Venereal infection eg Contagious Equine Metritis or Coital Eczema. | Antibiotic and antiseptic topical preparations. Apply Strict Code of Practice for hygiene. |
| **MASTITIS** Swelling in front of udder before foaling. | Fluid (oedema) normal. | No action required, will resolve after foaling. |
| Udder hot and hard one or both sides, mare may have temperature. | Mastitis due to bacterial infection eg Streptococcus or Staphylococcus infection. | Strip udder regularly of milk and insert intramammary antibiotic preparations. Mare may also need antibiotic injections. |
| Udder hot and hard wafter weaning. | May be mastitis but more likely normal until milk is reabsorbed. | No action required if no infection except to cut back on feed and give bran mash. |

| SIGNS OF DISEASE | CAUSES | TREATMENT AND PREVENTION |
|---|---|---|
| **LAMENESS**<br>Feet.<br>Acute lameness in one foot. | Foot abscess most likely cause. | Get vet or Farrier to check. Will need adequate drainage, antibiotic and tetanus prophylaxis from vet. |
| Acute lameness in front feet. | Laminitis most common cause due to overeating or toxaemia. | Pain killing drugs, warm water bathing. Surgical shoeing eg heart bar shoes.<br>Correct diet, check for intercurrent illness eg metritis. |
| Foot lameness chronic onset. | Consider Navicular Disease, Ringbone, fracture, pedal austerities. | All conditions like these need nerve blocks and X-rays for diagnosis. Vet required to diagnose and treat. |
| **LIMBS**<br>Sudden onset of lameness. | Injury eg fracture, nerve damage, puncture wounds. | All but most minor may require vet attention and tetanus prophylaxis. |
| Swelling down back of leg. | Tendon injury. | May need ultrasound for confirmation of diagnosis. Long rest required for treatment. |
| Slow onset, swollen joints. | Arthritis. Common in older horses and ponies. | Non-steroidal anti-inflammatory drugs eg phenylbutazone. |
| Fluid-filled limbs. | Sporadic lymphangitis ie Monday Morning Disease. Due to bad management ie too much feed and too little work. | Correct feed in relation to work. Diuretics are useful as treatment. |
| | Could be due to intercurrent disease eg Equine Arteritis or liver or heart failure or Purpura reaction after Strangles infection. | Check for other symptoms before considering treatment. Will need vet attention. |
| Generalised stiffness, reluctance to move. | Exertional Myopathy ie Tying Up or Azoturia. Due to exercise damage to muscles and faulty diet. | Non-steroidal anti-inflammatory products, electrolytes and correct diet. Complete rest. |
| **BEHAVIOUR**<br>Loss of appetite. | Any factor which causes a rise in temperature. Pain eg colic. | Further investigation required. See colic. |

99

| SIGNS OF DISEASE | CAUSES | TREATMENT AND PREVENTION |
|---|---|---|
| Spilling food from mouth. | Dental problems eg bad tooth or sharp edges to molars. | Teeth need rasping and checking at regular intervals ie every 6-12 months. |
| Nervous signs eg head pressing aimless wandering, aggression, unaware of surroundings. | Ragwort poisoning or chronic liver failure. | Nothing can be done. Euthanasia on welfare grounds. |
| Hindquarter weakness and paralysis. | Equine Herpes infection often after respiratory disease or abortion. | Corticosteroids may help but very poor prognosis. Strict hygiene required. Vaccine available. |
| Difficulty in walking, progressive stiffness, anxiety, 3rd eye lid prolapse, tetanic spasms and death. | Tetanus due to wound penetration (often not found) by Clostridium tetani. Toxins cause the symptoms. | High doses of antibiotic, tetanus antisera and sedation. Very poor prognosis. TETANUS VACCINATION IS A MUST FOR ALL HEALTHY HORSES AND PONIES. |
| **SUDDEN DEATH** | Anthrax NOTIFIABLE DISEASE AND INFECTIOUS TO PEOPLE. Due to infection by Bacillus anthracis. Rare in horses. | Sudden deaths must be investigated and if Anthrax is suspected or diagnosed then inform Divisional Veterinary officer. |
| Sudden death after or during exercise. | Rupture of major blood vessel and gross internal bleeding. | Nothing can be done to foresee such a catastrophe. |
| Sudden death after storm. | Lightning strike. | Scorch marks can often be seen on the animals hide. |
| | Plant poisoning eg Yew or Laurel. | Keep all animals away from hedge and tree clippings. |
| | Abdominal catastrophe after colic eg twisted bowel or ruptured stomach. | See section on colic for prevention. |
| | Acute Clostridial Disease. | Only Clostridial licensed vaccine for use in horses is against tetanus. |

# A GUIDE TO ANIMAL AILMENTS AND TREATMENT — FOALS

| SIGNS OF DISEASE | CAUSES | TREATMENT AND PREVENTION |
|---|---|---|
| **HEAD AND FACE** Nasal Discharge, thin, grey, one or two nostrils with cough. | Possible virus infection eg Equine Flu or Equine Herpes. | Antibiotic to protect against secondary pneumonia. Mucolytic and Bronchodilators. Good hygiene and nursing essential. Vaccine available against Equine Flu. |
| Milk coming down nostril when suckling in very young animal. | New born animal check for cleft palate. | Surgery is possible but guarded prognosis. |
| Food material coming down nostril in older foal. | Gullet choked with food material. | Most cases respond to sedatives and muscle relaxants. Severe cases may require stomach tube and syphoning. Usually occurs with dry food. |
| Yellow purulent discharge from one or nostrils. | Strangles due to Streptococcus equi or similar infection due to Streptococcus zooepidemicus. | Penicillin still drug of choice. Strict hygiene and isolation required. Very infectious. |
| Non-specific discharge. | Usually infection in upper respiratory tract or sinus due to a variety of bacteria. Consider also possibility of pneumonia if animal is breathing heavily. | Need nasal swab for diagnosis. Antibiotic and mucolytic helpful. Good nursing care and hygiene is a must. |
| Salivation and dribbling from the mouth. | Check for foreign body or damage due to trauma eg a kick. | If in doubt get vet to check. Most mouth sores will heal with salt water bathing and antibiotic. |
| | Mouth ulcers due to virus or bacterial infection. | Salt water bathing. Antibiotic may be necessary. |
| | Choked with food material. | See above. |

| SIGNS OF DISEASE | CAUSES | TREATMENT AND PREVENTION |
|---|---|---|
| Unable to swallow, dribbling with general stiffness. | Tetanus due to infection with Clostridium tetani. | High doses of antibiotic and antisera, sedatives. Very poor prognosis. Vaccine is a must in all healthy horses. |
| Loss of hair from face and muzzle. | Probably nothing wrong. Change of foal coat. | No action required. |
| Loss of hair with scabs. Round lesions. | Ringworm due to Trichophyton or Microsporum spp. CARE, INFECTIOUS TO PEOPLE. | Griseofulvin orally is best treatment but topical preparations can be used. |
| Sores and redness on white parts of face and muzzle. | Sunburn and or photosensitisation Eating some plants eg St John's Wort can predispose to condition. | Remove from sunlight. Use sun blockage eg Calamine on sore areas. |

**EYES**

| SIGNS OF DISEASE | CAUSES | TREATMENT AND PREVENTION |
|---|---|---|
| Discharge from one or both eyes. | Conjunctivitis due to bacterial infection. | Eye ointments or drops with antibiotic and steroids if directed by vet. |
| | Eye discharge may be part of other general infection eg Strangles or Flu. | Check for other symptoms before treatment. |
| Discharge from one eye. | Check for hay seed or similar in eye. Could be trauma. | Remove foreign body (usually job for the vet). Antibiotic eye ointment. |
| Swollen eye lids. | Could be just infection but allergic reaction should be considered. | Antibiotic, cortico-steroid or anti-histamine. If part of general reaction injections will be required. |
| Eyes dull and lifeless. | Animal may be in pain or have a general systemic illness. | Check for theory symptoms before treatment. If in doubt get vet. |
| Blindness with opacities in the eyes. | Congenital cataracts. | Consult vet. Probably poor prognosis. |
| Blindness with no apparent eye defects. | Diffuse or focal brain lesion eg abscess or tumour. | Nothing practical can be done. |

| SIGNS OF DISEASE | CAUSES | TREATMENT AND PREVENTION |
|---|---|---|
| Other nervous symptoms eg wandering, aggression, head pressing. | Acute Ragwort poisoning. | Nothing can be done. |
| Yellow colour in white of eye. | Jaundice due to liver disease or chronic Ragwort poisoning. | If disease due to infection antibiotic may be useful. Also high doses of Vitamins and extra carbohydrate in the feed. |
| Membranes of the eye pale and white. | Anaemia due to worms or lice or deficiency in the diet. | Make a definite diagnosis first then deworm or kill lice. Improve diet and give iron vitamin supplement. |
| | Very young foals consider Haemolytic Disease due to colostrum antibody destroying foals red blood cells. | Blood transfusion of compatible blood. Stop foal suckling mares colostrum for at least 48 hours. Give colostrum from another source. |
| Membranes of the eye dark and congested. | Circulatory problems as part of more general disease problem or colic or toxaemia. | Almost always a poor prognosis. Get vet to check and treat as matter of urgency. |
| Eyes sunk into eye sockets. | Dehydration usually caused by scouring. | Electrolytes as fluid replacement. Diagnose cause of scour eg worms or bacterial infection and treat accordingly. |
| **EARS** Discharge from one or both ears with head shaking. | Bacterial or mite infection. | Dog ear drops. Not licensed for use in horses but often used. |
| **SKIN AND HAIR** Coat colour changes with and without hair loss. | Probably changing from foal coat to adult. | Normal, no action required. |
| Loss of coat with wet crusty lesions on legs, back or on quarters. | Rain scald or Mud Fever due to Dermatrophilus infection. | Provide shelter to dry coat. Antibiotic may be necessary by injection or topically. Povidone iodine or chlorhexidine skin scrubs are useful. |

| SIGNS OF DISEASE | CAUSES | TREATMENT AND PREVENTION |
|---|---|---|
| Raised patch of hair with round dry crusty areas sometimes wet in the centre. | Ringworm due to Trichophyton or Microporum species. CARE, INFECTIOUS TO PEOPLE. | Topical antifungal agents or oral griseofulvin. Care, keep rugs and grooming equipment and tack disinfected to avoid spreading infection. |
| Loss of hair in mane and else where, parasites seen. | Ectoparasite eg lice. | Parasitic dusting powder or skin washes. |
| Raised sore areas on non-pigmented part of skin eg face and legs. | Photosensitisation due to sunlight. Animal is often made more susceptible by eating certain plants eg St John's Wort. | Remove from direct sunlight. Sun block creams or calamine lotion may be useful. May be necessary to protect area from flies. |
| Small growths on skin surface particularly around the muzzle. | Warts due to virus infection. | No action required. Will self-cure. |
| Small eggs deposited on hairs of neck and legs in late summer and autumn. | Bot eggs deposited by Gastirophilus species. | These can be difficult to remove. Deworm foal November to January using wormer with boticidal action. |

**BREATHING**

| | | |
|---|---|---|
| Rapid breathing. | Pneumonia due to virus eg Flu or Herpes infection and then secondary bacterial infection. | Antibiotic and anti-inflammatory drugs. Careful nursing and good ventilation essential. |
| | Stress due to pain, heat or over exercise. | Remove source of stress and condition should resolve quickly. |
| Dry coughing. | Respiratory infection most commonly due to virus infection eg Flu or Herpes. | Treat symptoms with Brochodilating and mucolytic drugs. Antibiotic to protect against secondary infections. Vaccine available against Flu. Herpes vaccine not effective against respiratory infection. |
| Soft cough. | Bacterial infection eg Strep. equi or S. zooepidemicus. | Penicillin is still drug of choice. Strict isolation of infected animal(s) and disinfect tack, stables and equipment. |

| SIGNS OF DISEASE | CAUSES | TREATMENT AND PREVENTION |
|---|---|---|
| Chronic cough. | Lung worm infection. Still common when grazed with donkeys. | Febendazole and Ivermectin are both effective drugs. |

**TEMPERATURE**
Normal is 100.5 F

| | | |
|---|---|---|
| Raised. | Usually means animal has an infection but can be result of pain eg colic or stress or exercise. | Diagnosis needs to be made. If in doubt see vet. If due to exercise or heat stress, rub down and symptoms should disappear. |
| Lowered. | Check reading again, may be faulty technique. Very young foal may be the result adverse weather conditions and lack of food (colostrum). | If correct raise body temperature by means of heat lamps, rub down and cover with rug. Check to make sure animal is feeding. |
| | Foal may be in terminal decline, possibly due to scouring. | Get vet assistance ASAP. |
| Sweating. | Unlikely to be due to fever. More likely due to exercise stress or colic. | Check for other symptoms. Any signs of pain get vet. Rub down vigorously with hay wisp. |
| Shivering. | Might be just inclement weather but not if indoors. See above for lowered temperature. | Mild shivering due to adverse weather and or lack of food can be quickly rectified by shelter and feeding. If not resolving quickly, get vet. |

**DUNG**

| | | |
|---|---|---|
| Constipation. | Retained meconium very common problem in first few days of life. | Soapy water or liquid paraffin enemas. Liquid paraffin by mouth. If severe vet may need to remove manually. |

**SCOURING**

| | | |
|---|---|---|
| Milk diarrhoea, yellow or white in colour. | Foal heat diarrhoea. Seen at mares first season after foaling. | Most get better without treatment. Kaolin bismuth mixtures may be useful. |
| | Strongyloides westeri infection from larvae in mare's milk. | Deworm foal with Fenbdendozle or Ivermectin or Pyrantel or similar products. |

| SIGNS OF DISEASE | CAUSES | TREATMENT AND PREVENTION |
|---|---|---|
| Profuse diarrhoea, often like water. Animal very depressed. | Bacterial infection eg E. coli or Shigella infection. Rotavirus may be involved as well. | Antibiotic, electrolytes and good nursing care. |
| Profuse diarrhoea with some blood. | Salmonellosis ie infection by one of the Salmonella species. CARE, COULD BE INFECTIOUS TO PEOPLE. | Antibiotic, electrolytes and good nursing care. Isolate cases and apply strict hygiene precautions. |

## URINARY SYSTEM

| | | |
|---|---|---|
| Repeated straining to pass urine. | Cystitis or urethral blockage very unlikely in foal. Symptoms more likely due to constipation. | Need vet to check before attempting treatment. |
| Urine dribbling from navel region. | Patent urachus. Congenital defect. | Poor prognosis. Surgery may be indicated. May occasionally rectify as the foal grows. |
| Abdominal pain/Colic. Seen as lack of appetite, groaning, sweating, kicking at belly, rolling etc. | In foal most likely due to meconium retention ie constipation, but could be due to worms or internal catastrophe such as twisted bowel. | Stop patient from rolling until the vet arrives by keeping it on its feet by walking it. If constipation vet may use enema or drench by stomach tube. Pain killing, antispasmodic and sedative injections may be used. If vet diagnosis twisted bowel or similar patient will need emergency surgery or euthanasia. |

## LAMENESS FEET

| | | |
|---|---|---|
| Heat and pain in one foot. | Abscess, as the result of infection penetrating through a crack in hoof wall or sole. | Pare foot to allow drainage and then poultice. Antibiotic and tetanus antiserum or vaccine. |
| Upright front foot different in conformation to the other (Boxy foot.) | Contracted tendons. Usually congenital problem which appears in first few months of age. | Minor cases can be rectified by Farrier by corrective trimming and shoeing. If severe problem, surgery may be indicated. |
| Smell and foul discharge from around the frog. | Thrush due to bacterial fungal and infection. | Clean foot and spray with antibiotic spray. Keep feet clean and dry as prevention. |

| SIGNS OF DISEASE | CAUSES | TREATMENT AND PREVENTION |
|---|---|---|
| Limbs | Injury eg fracture, nerve damage, puncture wounds and strains to muscle and tendons. | All but most minor will need vet diagnosis and attention. |
| Swollen and painful joint with temperature. | Joint ill due to bacterial infection usually from the navel. | Antibiotic in high doses. |
| Sore joint with swelling but no temperature. | Epiphysitis ie inflammation of the growth plates. Due to calcium phosphorous imbalance or foal being overweight. | Correct feed imbalance. Calcium, Vit D supplements. Get vet or nutritionist to check diet. |

**BEHAVIOUR**

| | | |
|---|---|---|
| Loss of appetite. | A rise in body temperature will normally cause lack of interest in feeding. Pain or colic constipation eg retained meconium. | Diagnosis needs to be established by vet if anorexia lasts more than a few hours. |
| Nervous symptoms within 24 hours of birth eg aimless movements or sleepiness, teeth grinding, barking noises. | Neonatal Maladjustment Syndrome (Barkers Wanderers, Dummy foals, Convulsive foals.) Cause not completely understood. | Nursing care. Sedation electrolytes and maintain body heat. Feed with stomach tube or bottle. |
| Foal born normal but within 24 hours becomes very weak, tired and reluctant to suck, no convulsions. | Haemolytic disease of the new-born foal. Due to antibody reaction to mare's colostrum. | Blood transfusions may be necessary. Muzzle foal for 36-48 hours and give colostrum from another mare. Avoid the same mating again. |
| Foal born weak and will not stand or suck properly. | Premature foal. | Good nursing and support care required. |
| Foal usually within three weeks of birth becoming very sleepy, usually with a temperature. | Septicaemia due to bacterial infection. Wide range of bacteria involved. | Antibiotic by injection which may have to be given intravenously. Electrolytes may be required. |

| SIGNS OF DISEASE | CAUSES | TREATMENT AND PREVENTION |
|---|---|---|
| Progressive onset of stiffness, unsteady gait, inability to swallow, convulsions. | Tetanus due to infection by Clostridium tetani. Entry of organism through a penetrating wound. | Tetanus antiserum, high doses of antibiotic and sedation. Very poor prognosis. Tetanus vaccination is effective and essential. |
| **SUDDEN DEATH** | Anthrax (NOTIFIABLE DISEASE) More rare in horses than cattle. Acute colic due to twisted gut or other abdominal catastrophe. | Wherever possible all cases of sudden death should be investigated properly by post mortem examination by a veterinary surgeon. |
| | Plant poisoning eg Yew Laurel Laburnum. | Never leave hedge or tree clippings accessible to livestock. Check all fences. |
| | Acute Clostridial infection. | Only Clostridial disease vaccine licensed in horses is against tetanus. |
| | Lightning strike or electrocution. | Lightning strike victims may have scorch marks on the skin with circumstantial evidence of a storm. GET QUALIFIED ELECTRICIAN TO CHECK ALL FITTINGS. |

# RABBITS

Rabbits are kept for many reasons. Most rabbits that the average vet will encounter are kept as pets, for show or for laboratory purposes, but they are assuming an increasing importance for meat and Angora wool production.

It is tempting to think that the only disease that a rabbit will encounter is Myxomatosis. This is without doubt the most important affliction that can overcome rabbits and against which the rabbit must be vaccinated. However, myxomatosis is only one of a host of diseases that a rabbit keeper and breeder must be on the alert against.

It is important that rabbits, as it is for any other group of farm animals, are well housed in comfortable, well ventilated quarters. Failure to house them properly will cause welfare and disease problems which, if the animals are kept commercially, can result in great economic losses.

Breeding and keeping rabbits on a commercial basis demands just as much care and attention to detail as keeping and breeding any other species. It is fairly specialised knowledge which the average farmer does not have and would be well advised to learn before embarking on a commercial rabbit enterprise.

# A GUIDE TO ANIMAL AILMENTS AND TREATMENT — RABBITS

| SIGNS OF DISEASE | CAUSES | TREATMENT AND PREVENTION |
|---|---|---|
| **HEAD AND FACE** | | |
| Nasal discharge often know as 'Snuffles'. | Upper respiratory infection eg Rhinitis, Sinusitis or pneumonia due to bacterial infection. Bacterial infection common due to Pasteurella or Staphylococcus or Pseudomonas Bordetella. | Medication with broad spectrum antibiotic. Isolate or eliminate infected animals. Check environment for ventilation, humidity and draughts. Vaccination against Pasteurella is possible. |
| Nasal discharge followed by eye discharge, and eye lid and head swelling. | Myxomatosis due to a Pox Virus infection. | Nothing can be done with the acute form of the disease. Euthanasia is only option. Vaccination is highly effective. |
| Salivation and dribbling from the mouth. | Irregular or sharp molars. | Will need teeth clipping or rasping. Needs to be done under general anaesthesia. See vet. |
| Loss of hair from head. | Ringworm due to infection by microsporum and Trichophyton species. CARE, INFECTIOUS TO PEOPLE. | Add Griseofulvin to the feed or can effect cure by spraying compartment with antifungal spray. Strict hygiene essential. |
| | Hair may be plucked by cage mates. | Isolate either victim or culprit. |
| | Hair may be lost by rubbing due to irritation from ear mites. | Check ears and treat with antibiotic and acaricide such as licensed for use in dogs and cats. Ivermectin may also be injected but dose needs to be regulated by vet. |
| **EYES** | | |
| Discharge from one or both eyes. | Early signs of Myxomatosis due to virus infection. | No treatment. |
| Discharge from one or both eyes with the rabbit remaining well otherwise. | Conjunctivitis due to bacterial infection. | Antibiotic eye ointment or drops. Check building for draughts and excessive ammonia concentrations. |

| SIGNS OF DISEASE | CAUSES | TREATMENT AND PREVENTION |
|---|---|---|
| Nodules on eye lids. | Nodular form of Myxomatosis. | Rabbits with this chronic form of Myxomatosis may survive. Antibiotic eye ointment or drops may help local symptoms. |
| Swollen eye lids. | Myxomatosis. | See above. |
| Eyes dull and lifeless. | Part of any general debilitating disease. | Check for other symptoms before beginning treatment. |
| Eyes opaque. | Cataracts due to congenital usually inherited, defects. | Nothing practical can be done. |
| Blindness, eyes looking normal. | Disturbance in the Central Nervous System. | Nothing practical can be done. |
| Yellow colour in the white of the eye. | Jaundice due to liver disease eg Liver Fluke infection (rare) or liver abscess due to bacterial infection. | Jaundice in rabbits is quite rare and the cause of the disease should be known before treatment is carried out. Poor prognosis. |
| Mucosa of the eye pale or white. | Anaemia due to internal haemorrhage or internal parasites eg worms or fluke. Also haemorrhagic gastroenteritis due to bacterial infection. | Vitamin supplements and iron injection. Anthelmintic after determining type of parasite by examining faecal sample. |
| Mucosa of the eye dark and congested. | Circulatory problems as part of more general disease process eg pneumonia or toxaemia. | Treat for general symptoms. Will need vet. |
| Eyes sunk into sockets. | Acute dehydration usually the result of diarrhoea. This can be due to bacterial, viral or parasitic infection. | Electrolytes and good nursing care. Treat cause of diarrhoea. May require faecal sample test. |

**EARS**

| | | |
|---|---|---|
| One or both ears swollen. | Abscess or haematoma (blood blister) due to injury. | Lance and drain abscess and give antibiotic. Often better to leave haematoma to absorb naturally. |

| SIGNS OF DISEASE | CAUSES | TREATMENT AND PREVENTION |
|---|---|---|
| Dry crusts in ears. | Ear mites due to infection by Psoroptes cuniculi. | Antibiotic acaricidal ear preparations normally used for dogs and cats can be used. Ivermectin injection also very successful. |
| One ear drooping with purulent discharge. | Bacterial infection, could be a number of different bacteria involved. | Antibiotic eg oxytetracycline. |

## SKIN AND HAIR

| | | |
|---|---|---|
| Self plucking of hair. | Physiological reason. Does pluck hair before giving birth to line nest. | Normal, no action required. |
| Hair chewing and plucking by litter mates. | Due to boredom or other stress factors. | Provide more hay and straw. Reduce light intensity and isolate the offender. |
| Partial hair loss mostly over head, ears and paws. Skin dry and itchy. | Ringworm due to Microsporum and Trichophyton species. CARE, INFECTIOUS TO PEOPLE. | Add Griseofulvin to the feed. Strict hygiene required to stop infection to other animals. Do not feed to pregnant animals. |
| Large soft swellings on head and other parts of body. | Abscesses due to bacterial infection. eg Pasteurella or Staphylococcus species. | Lance and drain and rinse with antiseptic or antibiotic solution. |
| Wet purulent patches on skin and udder. | Bacterial skin infection due to Staphylococcus or Pseudomanas species. | Topical and oral antibiotic treatment required. Check management to ensure clean and dry pens. |
| Generalised itching with hair loss, parasites seen under magnification or naked eye. | Fur mites eg Cheyletiella or Listrophorus species. Fowl red mite is also possibility. Lice and fleas are rare. | Treat topically with an insecticide such as are approved for use in dogs and cats. Dichlorvos strips hanging in shed may act as prevention. |
| Raised nodular swellings over head, ears, nose and paws. | Chronic form of Myxomatosis. | No treatment although some rabbits can survive this form of the disease. |

| SIGNS OF DISEASE | CAUSES | TREATMENT AND PREVENTION |
|---|---|---|
| Sore and swollen hocks and feet. | Ulcerative Pododermatitis due to infected pressure sores. | Antibiotic and good nursing care. House on thick dry straw. |

**BREATHING**

| | | |
|---|---|---|
| Rapid breathing. | Pneumonia due to bacterial or viral infection. Pasteurella bacteria and Myxomatosis virus most commonly involved. | Antibiotic by injection or in feed or water.<br><br>Check ventilation, get rid of draughts. |
| | Stress due to fear, pain or overheating. | Remove source of stress and symptoms should resolve quite quickly. |
| Snoring type of breathing. | Probable infection by Bordetella bronchiseptica. | Tetracycline antibiotic usually very effective. |
| Shallow, light breathing. | Probably just asleep but if unable to waken may be terminal decline. | Check for other symptoms and if necessary get the vet. |

**TEMPERATURE**
Normal range is 102 - 102.5 F ie 39.5C.

| | | |
|---|---|---|
| Raised. | Usually means the animal has an infection eg pneumonia or mastitis but it can be due to pain or stress or hot weather. | Antibiotic required for any infection once diagnosed but check external environmental factors. |
| Lowered. | Check again, may be due to incorrect technique. Hypothermia or terminally ill. | Check again for other symptoms eg diarrhoea. Raise body temperature with lamps and give good thick straw bed. |

**FAECES**

| | | |
|---|---|---|
| Constipation. | Rarely a problem but long haired rabbits do suffer from hair balls ingested when grooming. | Dose with liquid paraffin once or twice a day until the problem is resolved. |
| Constipation or impaction in the caecum(digestive organ). | Mucoid enteritis or enteropathy. Cause still obscure but may be bacterial | Antibiotic and corticosteroid may help. Tetracyclines said to be effective in prevention. |

| SIGNS OF DISEASE | CAUSES | TREATMENT AND PREVENTION |
|---|---|---|
| Diarrhoea in young rabbits, often watery and yellow. | E. coli infection. | Antibiotic usually neomycin most effective. good nursing care essential in the very young. Cleanliness and good hygiene essential in limiting outbreaks. |
| Diarrhoea, usually 5-6 weeks old rabbits, sometimes with blood and mucus. | Clostridial entero toxaemia. Due to spontaneous infection or administration of toxic antibiotic. | Broad spectrum antibiotic eg tetracyclines may be some use but very poor prognosis. |
| Acute diarrhoea with depression and high mortality rate. | Tyzzer's disease due to Bacillus piliformis. | Isolate all affected animals. Treat with tetracyclines. Thorough cleansing and disinfection required after outbreak/. |
| Chronic diarrhoea in any age of rabbit but most common in the young. | Viral diarrhoea and mucoid enteritis. Coccidiosis due to infection by Eimeria species of protozoa. | Antibiotic and electrolytes may be useful. Coccidiostats in the feed or water eg most sulphonamide preparations. Keep rabbits as clean and dry as possible as infection is picked up from litter. |

**URINE**

| | | |
|---|---|---|
| Discoloured urine. | Blood in urine due to bladder or kidney infection. May be discoloured by something the rabbit has eaten eg Beetroot. | Antibiotic, which needs to be prescribed by vet. No action required. Change the food and the discolouration should go quickly. |
| Straining to pass urine. | Possible bladder stone. Need X-ray to confirm. Consider possibility of difficulty in giving birth but this is much more rare. | Surgery usually required to remove stone. Careful examination required and referral to vet if necessary. |
| Purulent discharge from vulva, patient usually unwell. | Metritis ie infection of the uterus which may also be due retained foetus. | Antibiotic always required to clear infection. Prognosis always guarded especially for future breeding. |

| SIGNS OF DISEASE | CAUSES | TREATMENT AND PREVENTION |
|---|---|---|
| **LAMENESS** Feet and Legs. | Ulcers and sores on foot pad(s) and on hocks. Due to bacterial infection and poor management. | Antibiotic will heal the infection but pay attention to floor and bedding. Floor and bedding (thick straw) should be clean and dry. |
| | Injury eg fracture or strain common due to poor handling or rabbit leaping about. | All but the most minor will need vet attention. Fracture cases difficult to manage. |
| Hind leg paralysis. | Usually due to fracture of the spine. Result of bad handling but can occur with rabbit leaping about in play. | Nothing can be done. Euthanasia on welfare grounds. |
| **INFERTILITY** FEMALE Anoestrus ie failure to allow mating or not becoming pregnant after mating. | Moulting season or insufficient daylight hours. Extreme temperatures (hot or cold) or feeding inadequacies may also be factors. Overweight females may also show anoestrus. | Constant length of daylight hours and placing buck in vicinity of females. Make sure the breeding females are not too old or too fat. |
| Abortion. | Almost always due to bacterial infection eg Salmonella or Listerella species CARE, COULD BE INFECTIOUS TO PEOPLE. | Dot not treat Salmonella infections as animal may become a carrier. Tetracylines are effective against Listeriosis. |
| Death among newly born, including cannibalism. | Mostly due to defective mothering. Anoestrus may be a factor as well as housing and management. Some mothering instinct may be inherited. | Females should be allowed to nest in small, dark, well strawed boxes. AVOID HUMAN CONTACT. |
| | Hypothermia. New born rabbits are born naked and very sensitive to the cold. | Make sure nest box is well insulated and plenty of straw is provided. |
| Vaginal discharge. | Metritis due to bacterial infection. May also be retained dead foetuses. | Antibiotic and uterine irrigation. Remove dead foetuses. |

| SIGNS OF DISEASE | CAUSES | TREATMENT AND PREVENTION |
|---|---|---|
| **INFERTILITY** MALE | Congenital ie inherited and detected by keeping good records. | Nothing can be done. |
| | Infection in the testicles can cause sterility. | Unlikely that any treatment will be successful. |
| Hot and sore mammary gland(s). | Mastitis almost always due to Staphylococcus or Pasteurella species. | Antibiotic will resolve all but the most severe infection. |
| **BEHAVIOUR** Loss of appetite. | Any infection causing a rise in temperature. | Check for other symptoms before starting treatment. |
| | Dental abnormalities check mouth and teeth. | May require vet attention as molars may require filing under general anaesthetic. |
| Loss of appetite with teeth grinding. | Pain, particularly abdominal pain. May be due to hair balls or other intestinal obstruction. | Hair balls best treated with liquid paraffin. Oral dosing twice a day is needed. |
| Weight loss without diarrhoea. | Intestinal parasites ie worms Trichostrongyle and Oxyuris species most often involved. | Benzimidazole drugs (eg Panacur) most commonly used. |
| | Yersinia pseudotuberulosis. | Low doses of antibiotic eg chloramphenicol for up to a month. (not to be used for meat animals). |
| | Bacteria with rats and mice as carriers. | Rodent control essential. |
| | Hair balls. | Liquid paraffin. |
| Paralysis of hindquarters. | Almost always due to fracture of spine. | Nothing can be done euthanase on welfare grounds. |
| | Consider if X-ray is negative for spinal fracture Toxoplasma or Listerella infection. | Potentiated sulphonamides may work for Toxoplasma, Tetracyclines for Listerella infection. |
| Convulsions. | Epilepsy not uncommon in white breeds. May die during a convulsion. | Nothing practical can be done. |

| SIGNS OF DISEASE | CAUSES | TREATMENT AND PREVENTION |
|---|---|---|
| Twisted or wry neck. | Middle ear infection almost always due to Pasteurella multocida. | Antibiotic may stop the worst of the symptoms but prognosis generally poor. |
| Convulsions with twisted neck and paralysis. | Nosemosis ie infection by protozoan parasite. | Nothing effective can be done. |
| Splay leg. | Can occur in both front and hind legs and usually due to inherited defect. | Nothing practical can be done. Euthanase if problem is severe. Do not breed from affected animals. |
| After mating, buck falling off female and squealing in pain. | Normal behaviour. | No treatment. |
| **SUDDEN DEATH** | Any peracute systemic disease. eg Pasteurellosis. | No uncommon. All sudden deaths should be investigated in case other rabbits may be affected. Others at risk may be given antibiotic as a prevention. |
| | Heart failure. Not uncommon in older heavy animals. | Avoid obesity and lack of exercise. |

Also published by Smallholder Publications Ltd

*SMALLHOLDER* Magazine
The practical monthly for the small farmer

**First Catch Your Patient – A Vet on Call**
by R. Russell Lyon
*Experiences of a Fenland Vet*

# SMALLHOLDER PRACTICAL SERIES

**Introduction to Goatkeeping**
Jenny Neal

**Smallholders & Farmer's Legal Handbook**
by John Clarke

**Plain and Simple Egg Production**
by Carol Twinch

**So You Want to Keep Sheep**
by Carol Twinch

**Successful Lambing for the Small Flock Owner**
by John Bartelous

**Pig Rearing and Health**
by R. Russell Lyon

**A Guide to Angora-Cross Goats for Meat & Fibre**
by Joanna and David Charmain

**The Organic Grassland Smallholding**
by Jill Wolstenholme